NEW YORK

THE 400 RESTAURANTS THAT MATTER MOST

PETER & AMY MELTZER
JOHN F. MARIANI

Published by
Passport Press, Ltd.
P.O. Box 1980, New York, NY 10021
Tel: (212) 772-3942 Fax: (212) 535-8174
email: 76357.1561@compuserve.com

Cover: David Blumenthal-Creative Combinations Inc/FL
Maps: David Lindroth, Inc.
Typography: Fine Composition, Inc.
Printing: Montrose Publishing Co.

ISBN 0-937413-11-9

ABOUT THE AUTHORS

John Mariani has authored five books on American dining. His first, *The Dictionary of American Food and Drink* (revised, 1994, Hearst Books) was hailed as the "American Larousse Gastronomic." *America Eats Out*, (William Morrow 1991) won the International Association of Cooking Professionals award. His latest book, *The Four Seasons* was published by Crown in 1994. Currently, Mariani writes restaurant columns for *Esquire, Wine Spectator, Sports Afield, Diversion,* and *Cooking Light*. Further, he is restaurant expert for the PRODIGY Service.

Co-author Peter Meltzer is Publisher and Editor-in-Chief of *PASSPORT*. He has been tracking the restaurant scene since he began the *Wine Spectator's* "Grand Award Profiles," over a decade ago. Meltzer is presently a Contributing Authority to *Food Arts* magazine and also writes a bi-weekly column for *Wine Spectator*. In addition, Meltzer has co-hosted and co-directed the television and video pilots, "The Wine Magazine" and "Les Grands Chefs."

Amy Meltzer has a background in tabletop design and interiors. For several years, she was the Tabletop Editor for *Food Arts* magazine, and wrote a monthly column on table design for restaurants and hotels. She is President of Treasured Tabletops Inc., a company that creates individualized tablescapes for private clients and consults on the collection of table-top accessories.

CONTENTS

INTRODUCTION

Make the right choice every time you dine out! In this, the 11th edition of *PASSPORT*, we have focused our reviewing efforts more than ever before on the Manhattan restaurants that matter most. Between the countless deletions, additions and revisions to the latest edition, we believe that the places that have made it into the *PASSPORT 400* represent the very best in terms of quality, creativity, atmosphere, and value—at all levels.

The remarkable resource New York possesses is not its sheer number of restaurants, but the number of qualified chefs who have trained at culinary institutes and apprenticed at top establishments before venturing out on their own. They are preparing the kind of food that would instantly put them in the top percentile in any other city, whereas in Manhattan, there's a good chance you'll find an Aureole, Daniel or Lespinasse alumni presiding over a neighborhood bistro. We salute New York City's culinary excellence.

HOW TO USE THIS BOOK

All the restaurants in PASSPORT are laid out alphabetically by neighborhood. Headers at the top of each page indicate location. Six maps further pinpoint a restaurant's position. Alternatively, check our alphabetical listing. If you want to choose a restaurant by cuisine, consult our Food Index. If you are looking for bargains, consult our back-of-the-book index which designates dozens of great values. Sunday Suggestions, Fun Spots for Kids, Open Late, Winning Wine Lists, Take-out, and Destination Dining further facilitate the selection process.

RATINGS & SYMBOLS

Food		Wine List
★★★★★	Extraordinary	🍷🍷🍷🍷🍷
★★★★	Excellent	🍷🍷🍷🍷
★★★	Very Good	🍷🍷🍷
★★	Good	🍷🍷
★	Fair	🍷

$$$$$	$50 and up	$$	$20
$$$$	$40	$	$10
$$$	$30	½	$ 5

🍎 A NYC institution or special place—although not necessarily for the food.

PRICES

Our dollar signs refer to the cost of a dinner without wine or liquor, before tax and tip. Since the price of a bottle of wine can vary from $20 to well over $200, with an additional 25% to cover tip and tax, it is impossible to predict the full cost of a meal. Dinner for two can run from as little as $40 at a modest restaurant to upwards of $300 at a fancy one. Expect to pay about $80–$100 a couple on the average.

MORE ON PRICES

Prices for lunch tend to be much lower than dinner at stellar spots, so that you can dine regally at many deluxe restaurants for as little as $20 per person at lunch, whereas that same meal might cost you $60 at dinner. Beware of supplements on otherwise fixed price menus which can spoil a bargain meal.

RESERVATIONS

Don't show up without a reservation, particularly at top-rated restaurants and trendy destinations where you are expected to book way in advance. However, weekdays are easier than weekends and lunch easier still. You'd also be surprised how many times no-shows open up a table even on a Saturday night, so it's worth a last-minute call to find out. Another ploy is to book early (say, 6:00 PM) or quite late (9:30 PM). Always phone when you intend to cancel.

HOURS OF BUSINESS

Many of the restaurants reviewed in PASSPORT serve lunch and dinner seven days a week. An examination of all the establishments listed here showed that over 250 were open on Sunday alone. (See our index for recommendations.) But since days and even hours of business are subject to change, be sure to double-check.

DRESS

NYC restaurants tend to be fairly formal, so that a suit, or jacket and tie are recommended in midtown and the Upper East Side. In the Village, SoHo and TriBeCa, and many ethnic restaurants, dress tends to be more casual.

SMOKING, SEATING & SIBERIA

New York City law now bans smoking in all restaurants with more than 35 seats, unless the establishment offers a free-standing smoking room. Many people worry about another aspect of the "seating game" in deluxe or trendy restaurants, namely, who gets the best tables and how to avoid getting placed in "Siberia." "A" tables are customarily doled out to regular customers or celebrities, while newcomers may be seated elsewhere. Getting a "B" table is not a deliberate slight.

If you do get a bad table, request another. If available, the maître d' should move you to a better seat. Whatever you do, do not grease the palm of the maître d' on the spot. If you have gotten good service and liked where the maître d' seated you, you may choose to give him a tip ($10–$20 is fairly standard) on the way out.

TIPS ON TIPPING

Standard tip is 15% to 20% of the bill, pre-tax. Double the NYC sales tax, and you'll get the figure for a 16.5% tip. Most service staffs pool their tips at the end of each evening (busboys and bartenders are given a share), so it is not necessary to separate your tip in cash or on your credit card. If you do want to separate your tip in a deluxe restaurant, give 15% to the waiter and 5% to the captain.

Wine stewards are tipped only if they perform a special service, like decanting a rare wine or advising you throughout a multi-course meal. Then a tip of a few dollars (more still if you have uncorked a series of stellar vintages) is in order. Coat-check attendants usually get a dollar per coat. At the bar, tip a dollar on a $5–$10 drink order.

WATER WORKS

In some restaurants, bottled water—sparkling or still—can cost as much as a glass of wine. It is worth considering tap water as a serious alternative, especially since New York City water has scored particularly well in blind tastings.

CREDIT CARDS

Unless otherwise indicated, the restaurants listed in PASSPORT accept all major credit cards.

CUSTOMIZED PASSPORTS

PASSPORT TO NEW YORK, THE 400 RESTAURANTS THAT MATTER MOST is also available in customized editions imprinted with a corporate logo on the outside front cover and detailed text on the back cover. Volume discounts apply. For information, see order form in the center of this book, or telephone (212) 772-3942, fax (212) 535-8174.

ALPHABETICAL INDEX

PASSPORT PREVIEWS

BALTHAZAR—80 Spring Street (between Crosby and Broadway)—965-1414—Seasoned restaurateur Keith McNally and designer Ian McPheely have created a 160-seat brasserie with a turn-of-the-century look. It will feature a French country menu with entrees in the $13–$26 range, plus an oyster bar. Highlights include a 26-foot long pewter bar and an in-house bakery. Balthazar will serve lunch and dinner, and will stay open well past midnight.

IL CAMBIO—4 World Trade Center—Tony May (San Domenico, q.v.) is venturing downtown to debut a large, 9,500-square foot restaurant. More casual in look and feel than his elegant uptown ristorante, it will be divided into a traditional trattoria with a "tavola calda" (upscale fast food section) plus a self-service counter in a downstairs space. Chef Umberto Mombana, ex-Rex in L.A. and The Ritz Carlton in Hong Kong, will preside over the kitchen.

JEAN-GEORGES—1 Central Park West (in the Trump International Hotel) at 60th Street—299-3900—"This is the kind of place that you open once in a life-time," enthuses chef Jean-Georges Vongerichten (JoJo and Vong, q.v.) of his stunning, 70-seat installation with panoramic views of Central Park. The dining room, done in subtle hues of beige and gray, is an homage to clean geometric lines. Stark, high-backed chairs contrast with plush banquettes. A juxtaposition of Art Deco and contemporary elements, dramatic lighting and chic platinum tableware, the restaurant is a triumph for designer Adam Tihany. As for the menu, Vongerichten admits, "There's no new fish coming out of the sea," but he has been experimenting with a variety of exotic wild herbs such as wood sorrel and yarrow, which will be incorporated into traditional French recipes. He also expects to re-introduce *guéridon* service, with a number of dishes to be finished table-side. Patissier Eric Hubert will oversee the pastry operation. The average check will run about $65 per person. Jean-Georges serves dinner only, but breakfast and lunch are available in the adjacent café. Terrace dining in season.

PASSPORT PREVIEWS

LE CIRQUE 2000—455 Madison Avenue (between 50th and 51st Streets in the New York Palace Hotel)—794-9292—According to owner Sirio Maccioni, this will not be a simple reincarnation of the old Le Cirque (except for the prices, which he hopes to maintain at the old levels). Instead, the fanciful Adam Tihany design, which takes up three floors, incorporates a complete restoration of the landmark Villard rooms (created by Stanford White in 1882). It will feature a 120-seat restaurant and an open kitchen, as well as a dine-in wine cellar that accommodates 20, a separate cigar lounge, a full-scale bar, two private dining rooms seating a total of 200 and courtyard dining in season. In the main dining room, Tihany installed colorful and high banquettes, subtle overhead lighting and oversized etched-glass panels. Executive chef Sottha Khunn, who for years was Le Cirque's chef de cuisine, intends to prepare Le Cirque classics like bass in a potato crust, bolito misto and bouillabaisse with a contemporary twist, using less fat and butter. He will introduce some new Pacific Rim elements to the menu, along with some spicy curry recipes which Maccioni himself uncovered in Italy. Expect wonderful desserts from pastry chef Jacques Torres.

MONZU—142 Mercer Street (between Prince and Mercer Streets)—925-3700—Chef/owner Matthew Kenney's (Matthew's, Mezze, q.v.) latest undertaking takes its name from the Napoleonic chefs who ventured to Sicily to cook in the early 1800s. The upscale, 200-seat restaurant will showcase Sicilian produce and recipes. "Sicilian flavor combinations are amazing," says Kenney, "similar to Moroccan but entirely different in cooking style." Expect lots of roasted preparations, the likes of sweet and sour onions, bread salad with pomegranate, saffron-based pastas, and thinly sliced swordfish rolled with bread crumbs and pine nuts. The projected check is $45 with wine.

PASTIS—119 West 56th West (in the Parker Meridien Hotel)—751-2931—Chef David Ruggiero (Le Chantilly, Bistro de Maxim, q.v.) is opening a Mediterranean-style restaurant, with a whimsical design and an open kitchen, created by David Rockwell. The 90-seat restaurant will emphasize the cuisine of Southern France, with borrowings from Italy, North Africa and Greece. The projected check is in the $45 range.

PAYARD PATISSERIE & BISTRO—1032 Lexington Avenue (between 73rd and 74th Streets)—717-2766—Pastry chef François Payard and chef Daniel Boulud (both of Restaurant Daniel, q.v.) are opening a classic French patisserie and bistro designed by David Rockwell. Philippe Bertineau (ex Daniel) will be chef de cuisine. A third of the space will be devoted to delectable cakes, pastries, ice cream and sweets. There will be a 60-seat dining area in back, and additional seating for 40 on the mezzanine. The bistro will stay open all day, beginning with breakfast at 7:00 AM. At lunch, the emphasis will be on affordable light fare—sandwiches, salads and plats du jour. In mid-afternoon, there will be a traditional tea service. The dinner menu will feature classic French preparations like steak frites, roasted guinea hen with mushrooms, and poached skate. Lunch should cost $20–$25, with dinner running about $40–$45 including wine. "We want this to be a neighborhood place, not just a social hangout," says Boulud.

LOWER MANHATTAN

Ⓞ★★ **FRAUNCES TAVERN**—54 Pearl Street (at Broad Street)—269-0144—This landmark brick tavern, opened in 1762, is one of the city's true gems. It was here George Washington bade farewell to his troops in 1783. (Do visit the Colonial museum upstairs if time permits.) With its warm woods, worn leathers, faded flags and mounted trophies, you can't help but feel the ghosts of a vanished era. Slow service and a low-key atmosphere make this a quiet sanctuary well removed from Wall Street. Food and drink are homey and simply executed. Applewood-smoked salmon, grilled vegetable and goat cheese tart, Colonial New England clam chowder, Maryland crab cakes, baked chicken Washington, beef Wellington, Hannah Dair's baked apple crunch, cheesecake, chocolate banana cream pie. $$$$ 🍷🍷

★★★½ **HUDSON RIVER CLUB**—4 World Financial Center (at West Street)—786-1500—The loss of chef Waldy Malouf to the Rainbow Room (q.v.) has not put a damper on this spectacularly situated restaurant on the river, which offers a superb view of New York just above sea level. Comfortable but sedate, with very efficient service, this remains an ideal spot for a business meal. The Club (which it is not) has always featured the food and wines of the Hudson Valley, and new chef Jim Porteus is maintaining the tradition. Apple and butternut squash soup, ring-necked pheasant with braised apples and cabbage, braised venison pie, striped bass with Swiss chard and grilled corn in tomato broth, huckleberry crisps with maple ice cream, gingerbread cobbler. $$$$$ 🍷🍷🍷🍷

Ⓞ **SOUTH STREET SEAPORT**—This is not a restaurant but an historic district (that stretches from Fulton to Dover Streets) impeccably restored to its 19th-C. maritime grandeur, and it is very entertaining to explore. Lunch or dinner at one of the many restaurants here is also something of an adventure. You can expect to find a host of rather average fast food boutiques serving every imaginable type of ethnic cooking. Best bet is Sloppy Louie's, a charming old place, dating from 1874, which specializes in a diverse selection of fresh seafood. Very casual, with polite service, though a bit touristy. $$$ 🍷🍷

LOWER MANHATTAN

1 Fraunces Tavern
2 Wall Street Kitchen & Bar
3 South Street Seaport
4 Windows on the World
5 Hudson River Club

TRIBECA

11 Salaam Bombay
12 Gigino
13 Duane Park Cafe
14 The Odeon
15 Zeppole
16 Chanterelle
17 Spartina
18 Tribeca Grill
19 Nobu
20 The Independent
21 Layla
22 El Teddy's
23 Arqua
24 Montrachet
25 City Wine & Cigar Company
26 Capsouto Freres

SOHO

31 Canal House
32 Lucky Strike
33 Jour et Nuit
34 Downtown
35 Alison on Dominick
36 Aqua Grill
37 Savore
38 Blue Ribbon
39 Barolo
40 Erizo Latino
41 Sanzin
42 Soho Steak
43 Omen Restaurant
44 Raoul's
45 Frontière
46 Le Pescadou
47 Provence
48 Jean Claude
49 Quilty's
50 Cub Room
51 Félix
52 SoHo Kitchen & Bar
53 Honmura An
54 Match
55 Jerry's
56 Savoy
57 Zoë
58 Pravda
59 Penang
60 Cendrillon
61 Sweet Ophelia's
62 Cascabel
63 The Kitchen Club

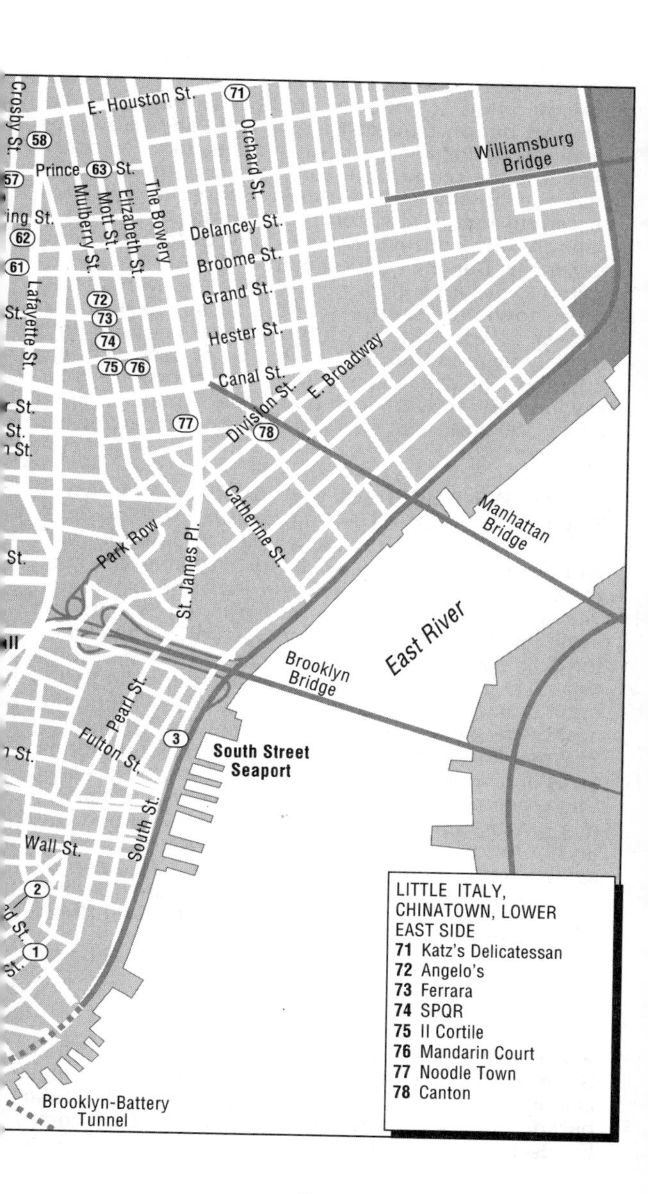
E. Houston St.
Crosby St.
Prince St.
Mulberry St.
Mott St.
Elizabeth St.
The Bowery
Orchard St.
Delancey St.
Broome St.
Grand St.
Hester St.
Canal St.
Division St.
E. Broadway
Lafayette St.
Williamsburg Bridge
Manhattan Bridge
Catherine St.
Park Row
St. James Pl.
Brooklyn Bridge
East River
Pearl St.
Fulton St.
South Street Seaport
South St.
Wall St.
Brooklyn-Battery Tunnel
LITTLE ITALY, CHINATOWN, LOWER EAST SIDE
71 Katz's Delicatessan
72 Angelo's
73 Ferrara
74 SPQR
75 Il Cortile
76 Mandarin Court
77 Noodle Town
78 Canton

LOWER MANHATTAN

★★½ **WALL STREET KITCHEN AND BAR**—70 Broad Street (near Beaver Street)—797-7070—With its narrow, winding streets, the neighborhood feels like London, but once inside this cramped and boisterous destination, you know you're in Manhattan. The popular bar is the centerpiece here, with a large autumnal photograph suspended above. Sponged walls in a matching leafy color complete the look. Service is friendly but frenzied. Owner Tony Goldman (Soho Kitchen & Bar q.v.) and chef Tom Valenti have conspired to deliver superior but casual fare, with a focus on sandwiches, burgers and pizzas. There's also Caesar salad, white bean dip, grilled sausage with lentils, steamed mussels, short ribs of beef with egg noodles. For dessert, old-fashioned chocolate cake, key lime pie. To wash it all down, there are 45 draught beers, 100 bottled varieties, and an extensive wine list. $$$ 🍷🍷🍷🍷

○ ★★★ **WINDOWS ON THE WORLD**—One World Trade Center—524-7000—You ascend 107 floors in 67 seconds. The elevator doors open to a 38-foot wall composed of 430,000 glass beads. Whether you head for the main dining room, the immodestly named "Greatest Bar on Earth," or "Cellar in the Sky" (where seven-course meals are matched with five fine wines for $125), you can see 90 miles in any direction on a clear day. Designed by the talented Hugh Hardy, the main dining room is an open space, done in a taupe and beige palette, with tableside service. Under chef Philippe Feret, the menu embraces an international array of bold flavors. Whole roasted foie gras glazed in Sauternes, grand shellfish platter, silver pot of seafood in a ginger broth, tureen of bouillabaisse topped with an entire lobster, squab roasted in rock salt, rack of spiced lamb, "chocolate delirium cake," all accompanied by a legendary wine list of more than 700 selections. "Sunset menu" (between 5:00 and 6:00 PM) is $35. $$$$$ 🍷🍷🍷🍷🍷

TRIBECA

★★★ **ARQUA**—281 Church Street (near White Street)—334-1888—Saffron colored rubbed walls, high ceilings, and huge paper lanterns create a dramatic backdrop for solid trattoria fare. Service is easy-going but decibels can be forbidding. Sautéed calamari, fresh pickled sardines, agnolotti with ricotta and goat cheese, Venetian fish soup, veal medallions with sage and white wine, spiced apple cake, raspberry and blueberry tart. $$$½ 🍷🍷

★★★½ **CAPSOUTO FRÈRES**—451 Washington Street (near Canal Street)—966-4900—Situated in a classically renovated, landmark building, with a view of the Hudson, the brothers Capsouto were among the first to offer Mediterranean and Provençal cuisine in what is now a benchmark by TriBeCa standards. French onion soup, smoked duck breast salad, sweetbreads with wild mushrooms, Nantucket bay scallops with lobster sauce, cassoulet of lamb, duck confit and pork loin, crème brûlée, quince tart with lavender. $$$$ 🍷🍷🍷

★★★★ **CHANTERELLE**—2 Harrison Street (at Hudson Street)—966-6960—Massive carved columns set against a backdrop of pale, peach-colored walls dominated by giant floral arrangements create a dramatic setting, amiably presided over by co-owner Karen Waltuck. Chef/co-owner David Waltuck's creations are highly flavorful in a subtle and refined manner. His presentation is equally effective. (However, in the Waltucks' absence, service can be very sluggish and the kitchen less than lustrous.) Chanterelle attracts a very loyal following despite the fact that its prices ($73 and $89 respectively for a three- and six-course fixed price dinner) are practically the highest in town. Ravioli of salmon and cabbage with black caviar, oysters with cream and truffles, squab with anise, grilled Arctic char, roasted venison with sauce poivrade, crisp chocolate soufflé cake, caramelized pear millefeuille, grapefruit soup and pomegranate. $$$$$ 🍷🍷🍷🍷

★★★ **CITY WINE & CIGAR COMPANY**—62 Laight Street (between Hudson and Greenwich Streets)—334-2274—This is the ultimate playground for the '90s. The sleek and glowing interior designed by Chris Williams, is resplendent with seductive architectural curves, buxom banquettes, reflecting tabletops and dramatic sculpted-glass fixtures. Smoking and drinking (as well as dining) are the main pursuits here—there is even a serious cigar boutique in case you forgot your Macanudos—although there is one room which is haven for those who do not indulge. Patricia Williams' hearty Southern-inspired fare includes clam fritters with herbed crema fresca, martini salad with gin-soaked olives and Maytag blue cheese, orange and jicama salad, ancho-rubbed chicken with hominy mole, black Angus steak with mashed potatoes, guava-glazed tuna, warm pear financier, hot chocolate cake, caramel crème anglaise. $$$½ 🍷🍷🍷

★★★½ **DUANE PARK CAFÉ**—157 Duane Street (between Hudson and West Broadway—732-5555—One of TriBeCa's most tranquil destinations, this relaxing and subdued room with tall black chairs, plump banquettes, rich woods and a draped ceiling conjures up both Asian and Italian design concepts. The menu is also a successful blend of the two cultures. The greeting and service are genuinely warm. Shrimp with mustard fruits, grilled miso duck, pappardelle with wild mushrooms, crispy skate with tempura vegetables, herb-crusted cod with rock shrimp and cannellini bean ragù, maple-roasted chicken stuffed with pecan risotto, banana-filled chocolate dacquoise, lemon-raspberry meringue tartlet, strawberry granita. Fixed price $19.97 lunch. $$$ 🍷🍷🍷

★★ **EL TEDDY'S**—219 West Broadway (between Franklin and White Streets)—941-7070—Lots of glitter and tile and whacky kinetic sculpture make this one of the city's more offbeat interiors. It's also one of the few spots where margaritas are made to measure with your choice of several different Tequilas. Queso fundido con choriso, shrimp tostada with jalapeno, grilled swordfish with Swiss chard, grilled pork loin with watercress and jicama, fire roasted corn. Sidewalk dining in season. $$½ 🍷🍷

★★★ **GIGINO**—323 Greenwich Street (between Duane and Reade Streets)—431-1112—This is a cheery, bustling, and airy trattoria. Atmosphere is casual and inviting; service is equally friendly. Shrimp in beer batter, barlotti beans with sausage and sage, ravioli alla sarda, spaghetti with beets, escarole and garlic, roasted free range chicken with cous cous. There are also a dozen different pizzas to contemplate, but do leave room for desserts like chocolate almond torte or Italian cheesecake. $$½ 🍷🍷

★★★ **THE INDEPENDENT**—179 West Broadway (between Leonard and Worth Streets)—219-2010—Named for the British newspaper, this Independent has a spirit all of its own—a handsome, two-storied space with brick walls, photographs, smartly-upholstered banquettes and two convivial bars. Service is upbeat and attentive. Chef Stephen Lyle, formerly of the Odeon, has long been an exponent of bistro fare with a particular knack for satisfying diverse palates. Caesar salad, grilled lamb sausage in a tortilla, roasted portabello mushroom with white beans, braised lamb with artichokes, roast beef with smoked onions and horseradish, roasted salmon with poblano salsa, warm apple tart, ginger cheesecake, banana split. $$$ 🍷🍷🍷

★★★½ **LAYLA**—211 West Broadway (near Franklin Street)—431-0700—Just a stone's throw away from Drew Nieporent's flagship Montrachet is his whimsical Middle Eastern outpost, done up in fanciful Arabian Night's fashion. The experience is highly entertaining, with a controversial belly dancer adding to the festivities. Chef Joseph Fortunato's food is seductively serious. You could easily feast on his delicious mezze, accompanied by home-baked pita bread: hummus, taramasalata, tabouleh, hot dolmas, cumin-spiced carrots, falafel, grilled octopus salad, Persian pizzas with spicy lamb. If you have room, there's excellent lobster pastilla with basmati rice, roasted cod fish with red lentil salad, spiced chicken with eggplant cakes, granita quince tart, orange blossom crème brûlée. Fixed price $28 dinner. $$$ 🍷🍷🍷

★★★★½ **MONTRACHET**—239 West Broadway (near White Street)—219-2777—Montrachet has taken on a patina of coziness with a pleasing array of paintings dotting the walls, dispelling the original, minimalist look. Staff is professional and attentive in every way without being obtrusive. Chris Gesualdi's Mediterranean-inspired food is excellent; Daniel Johnnes' wine list is legendary; why doesn't every neighborhood sport a place like this? Warm blue point oysters with Champagne sauce and osetra caviar, rabbit salad with roasted peppers, olives and basil, hot New York foie de canard with pear and huckleberry, seared sashimi tuna with sesame seaweed, medallion of veal with salsify and cèpes purée topped by red wine jus, truffle-crusted salmon, pintade with potatoes Anna, roasted chicken with potato purée and garlic sauce, quince tarte tatin, chocolate truffle torte with Grand Marnier ice cream, banana and chocolate gratin on linzer crust, crème brûlée. Degustation menus at $32, $38, and $65. $$$$ 🍷🍷🍷🍷🍷

TRIBECA

★★★★ **NOBU**—105 Hudson Street (corner of Franklin Street)—219-0500—Owned by superstar restaurateur Drew Nieporent, actor Robert DeNiro and celebrated chef Nobu Matsuhisa, this spot remains hotter than the earth's core. Designer David Rockwell's whimsical room of illuminated birch columns, blond woods and plush banquettes constantly fills with famous and fabulous faces who flock here to sample the exotic and original Japanese fare. A knowledgeable waiter or waitress will have a major impact on the rhythm of your meal, as the breadth of selection is considerable. Salmon tartare with caviar, toro tartare with caviar, monkfish paté, miso crisps with scallops, yellowtail with jalapeño, black cod in miso, soft shell crab roll, green tea mochi, plum and sake granité. $$$$ 🍷🍷🍷

★★ **THE ODEON**—145 West Broadway (at Thomas Street)—233-0507—Housed in a stylish Art Deco cafeteria, this was the first notable eatery in the TriBeCa neighborhood and the first to be adopted by the SoHo art set, which still makes it a major stamping ground after midnight. The Odeon has been enjoying a renaissance among a new set of night owls despite the departure of chef Stephen Lyle. Everybody here wears black, looks slightly world weary, and appears to know each other. The bistro fare is inconsistent, but the kitchen tries hard. Ricotta ravioli, grilled chicken with mashed potatoes and spinach, seared marinated tuna, lemon tart. $$$½ 🍷🍷🍷

★★ **SALAAM BOMBAY**—317 Greenwich Street (between Duane and Reade Streets)—226-9400—Here's an attractive, uptown-looking spot that seems out of place downtown. Service is well-intended, but painfully slow. Traditional appetizers like vegetable pakoras, kachori (dumplings), malai kofta (cheese and vegetable croquettes) and samosas lack punch, and entrees such as chicken tikka, seekh khabbab, korma lamb scallops lack finesse. $$½ 🍷

★★★½ **SPARTINA**—355 Greenwich Street (near Harrison Street)—274-9310—This is a casual and inviting place, unpretentious and moderately priced, with a menu that stresses the food of the French and Italian Riviera. Chef-owner Stephen Kalt is knowledgeable and creative, and has developed a strong following thanks to an original menu. Gnocchi "four ways," roasted beets with sweet onions, seared chicken livers with gorgonzola, tagliolini (with fresh tuna, capers, sun-dried tomatoes and black olives), Niçoise ravioli with Swiss chard, grilled shrimp on flatbread with warm potato salad, roasted cod with garlic mashed potatoes, chocolate soufflé, pistachio cherry baklava, Florentine apple tart. $$$½ 🍷🍷🍷

★★★½ **TRIBECA GRILL**—375 Greenwich Street (near Franklin Street)—941-3900—This striking space with exposed beams, high ceilings, brick walls and a lively bar scene is owned by Drew Nieporent, Robert DeNiro and a cast of celebrity partners. Convenient for a downtown lunch, at night it becomes a true destination. But the real star here remains the kitchen, under executive chef Don Pintabona and pastry chef George McCurdy, who ensure that you not only have a good time, but dine exceedingly well too. Crisp fried oysters, shrimp and vegetable spring roll, duck and foie gras paté, rare seared tuna with sesame noodles, chile-crusted chicken with spiced cornbread, herb-crusted rack of lamb with roasted vegetables, potato pancakes "Vonnas," banana tart with milk chocolate malt ice cream. The private dining room upstairs is ideal for a party. Fixed price $19.97 lunch. $$$$ 🍷🍷🍷

★★★ **ZEPPOLE**—186 Franklin Street (between Greenwich and Hudson Streets)—431-1114—This loud, vivacious and old-fashioned Italian-American restaurant is one of Drew Nieporent's latest undertakings. The concept is a throwback but hardly a feed hall. It's a big happy room (named after deep-fried Italian fritters), part bakery and part pizzeria, with large round tables, a bread pantry up front and enough vitality to power a Fellini movie. Chef Frank Crispo has a great sense of seasoning and David Norman is a talented baker, so from the first morsel of bread with olive oil to the last bite of biscotti and espresso, you'll be happy you came. Portions are large, meant to be enjoyed family style. Fennel and orange salad, braised artichoke with mint, rigatoni (with broccoli di rabe, provolone and sausage), tortelloni with Swiss chard and ricotta, chicken diavolo, sirloin with oregano topped by olive oil and lemon, TriBeCa chocolate torte, tiramisù, zeppole. $$$ 🍷🍷🍷

SOHO

★★★★ **ALISON ON DOMINICK**—38 Dominick Street (near Hudson Street)—727-1888—This intimate space with white walls, striking photographs, and navy blue banquettes has developed an exceedingly loyal following thanks to the efforts of tireless owner Alison Becker Hurt. (She also owns a restaurant in Sagaponack, L.I., called Alison by the Beach.) Chef Dan Silverman's French provincial menu is a winning departure from Alison's earlier Mediterranean slant. Foie gras glazed with balsamic vinegar, goat's cheese in crisp potato phyllo, roasted pheasant with Savoy cabbage, char with mushroom and artichokes, chocolate cake with pistachio ice cream and peaches, raspberry and lemon curd Napoleon. The extensive wine list also features some inexpensive French country bottlings that go well with this food. $$$$½ 🍷🍷🍷

★★★½ **AQUA GRILL**—210 Spring Street (at Avenue of the Americas)—274-0505—A winding, yellow-walled space packed with animated diners. Seashell lamp fixtures proclaim the menu's bountiful offering of seafood. Service is both professional and caring. Chef Jeremy Marshall's food is creative, complex and satisfying. Peppered tuna carpaccio, roasted crabcake Napoleon, Maine lobster salad, grilled Atlantic salmon with falafel crust, grilled swordfish with sautéed broccoli rape, grilled yellowfin tuna with pasta tapenade, molten chocolate souffle with coffee cream, roasted grapefruit with ruby red sorbet. Good wine by the glass program. Closed Monday. Fixed price lunch $14.50. $$$½ 🍷🍷🍷

★★ **BAROLO**—398 West Broadway (between Spring and Broome Streets)—226-1102—A striking example of contemporary Milanese design, this handsome, three-tiered restaurant also boasts a large garden for summer dining. The kitchen does not match the deftness of the interior design, but you can count on passable pastas and other staples like spinach flan, stuffed chicken breast, and grilled tuna. Service may be agonizingly slow. Great wine list. $$$ 🍷🍷🍷🍷

★★½ **BLUE RIBBON**—97 Sullivan Street (near Spring Street)—274-0404—A highly animated, casual spot that stays open very late, which has become something of an after-hours hang out for chefs whose restaurants close earlier. Chef-owner Eric Bromberg's menu is very eclectic: try the pu-pu platter of pierogies, grilled shrimp remoulade, chicken wings, egg rolls, and ribs for an inexpensive overview of his appetizers. Shrimp Provençal with ricotta ravioli, grilled striped bass with pearl onions, fried chicken with mashed potatoes and collard greens, chocolate Bruno. $$½ 🍷🍷

★★★ **CANAL HOUSE**—310 West Broadway (between Canal and Grand Streets)—965-3588—This austere room with faded sepia tones is tucked away on the parlor floor of the high-tech, retro-looking SoHo Grand Hotel. The mood is serene and low-key, but there are quirky touches of humor and flair. The menu lists a compendium of American favorites such as Caesar salad, fried calamari and shrimp, New England seafood chowder, macaroni and cheese, Yankee pot roast, grilled Long Island duck breast, pecan pie, butterscotch molasses pudding. $$$ 🍷🍷

★★★★ **CASCABEL**—218 Lafayette Street (between Broome and Spring Streets)—431-7300—This restaurant has truly come into its own. Vivid red walls hung with geometric mirrors, flickering votive candles and flamboyant upholstery have all taken on a richer patina. Chef Sam Hazen (formerly of Gavroche in London and Quatorze in New York) has elevated this Zaccaro–family owned spot to new heights with his intricate and sophisticated preparations that are presented with great style. The delightful staff is professional and discreet. Seared sea scallops with polenta croutons, graavlax with chickpea pancake and caviar, duck pastrami with cabbage salad, pan-seared halibut with truffled herb salad, lamb chops wrapped in root vegetables, pan-roasted duck breast with honey-glazed cippoline onions, new-fashioned baked Alaska, banana bombe, apple-cream cheese tart. The wine selections are highly original. $$$$ 🍷🍷🍷

★★★½ **CENDRILLON**—45 Mercer Street (between Broome and Grand Streets)—343-9012—Tucked away under a discreet sign on Mercer Street is this unassuming restaurant with warm brick walls, carved wooden tables, cozy banquettes and a convivial bar. Chef Romy Dorotan's open kitchen churns out a litany of creative Filipino dishes: Amy's spring roll, fresh lumpia with chicken saté, seared beef sambal with tomato fennel and beet salad, quail and rabbit adobo with mashed taro root, Romy's "Chinese smokehouse" spare ribs, Manila clams with leeks and shiitakes, shrimp curry with green chiles and okra, caramelized banana cake, peach bread pudding with vanilla ice cream. $$$ 🍷🍷🍷

★★★ **CUB ROOM**—313 Sullivan Street (at Prince Street)—677-4100—A hip and stylish space with one of the best-looking bars in the city. In name, the Cub Room recalls New York's Supper Club era, but Henry Meer's menu features inviting contemporary American fare: pressed vegetable terrine, salmon Caesar, grilled gulf shrimp with carrot and caraway sauce, wood-grilled lobster fricassée, chateaubriand with wild mushrooms, espresso granité. Prices are lower at the adjacent Cub Room Café, where you can dine on hanger steak, turkey pot pie or a "Cub Club." $$$ 🍷🍷🍷

★★ **DOWNTOWN**—376 West Broadway (at Broome Street)—343-0999—A SoHo outpost of the celebrated Harry's Bar in Venice (the New York flagship, Harry Cipriani, is on Fifth Avenue and 59th Street) that draws sleek and fashionable patrons who come to eat the famous carpaccio and sip the outrageously expensive bellinis. It is a stunning space with a grand Venetian chandelier, dramatic black-and-white canvasses offset by deep yellow walls and modern leather chairs. Would that the food had the sublime edge of the Cipriani's other restaurants, but here most of it seems mundane. Scallops with artichokes, risotto alla primavera, tagliarine gratinata, lemon meringue pie. Smokers seem to find a haven here in flagrant violation of NYC regulations. Fixed price dinner $28. $$$$ 🍷🍷

★★½ **ERIZO LATINO**—422 West Broadway (near Spring Street)—941-5811—Chef/proprietor Alex Garcia (formerly sous-chef at Patria) has devised an extensive, and somewhat rustic Latin American menu that nicely suits this casual downtown spot. The best time to sample his menu is at lunch, when overcrowding is rarely a problem. Mango and ginger soup, wild mushroom tamale, manchego cheese empanada, tangerine-glazed tuna, cumin-scented beef tenderloin, flourless hot chocolate pudding, caramelized coconut cream, tres leches (three-milk soaked orange sponge cake). Fixed price lunch $19.97. $$$ 🍷🍷

★★★ **FÉLIX**—340 West Broadway (corner of Grand Street)—431-0021—This handsome bistro with blond woods, mirrored walls and an imposing bar was renowned as a smoky singles' spot specializing in steak frites and a large dose of Gallic hauteur. Now the greeting and service are far more cordial and the whiff of Gitanes is limited to the bar area only. Thanks to the arrival of chef Renaud Le Rasle, who trained in Paris and at La Côte Basque, the food is much improved. Tuna and salmon tartare, country terrine, artichoke stuffed with mushrooms and sage, roasted cod with lentils and smoked salmon, braised lamb shank, rabbit stew in red wine sauce, cheesecake with orange marmalade, poached pear in red wine. Amex only. $$$ 🍷🍷

★★ **FRONTIÈRE**—199 Prince Street (near MacDougal Street)—387-0898—Very much a neighborhood meeting place with distressed walls, windows that open onto the street, and some good, not great, Provençal food. We found many of the textures off—marinated mackerel a bit dry, soft shell crabs too soft, profiteroles dense—but enjoyed the French sausage and frisée with goat's cheese, the medallions of lamb and the crème brûlée. Frontière organizes some good wine promotions. $$$ 🍷🍷🍷

★★★★ **HONMURA AN**—170 Mercer Street (between Houston and Prince Streets)—334-5253—Walk up a flight of stairs and into an engaging, airy and tranquil space with brick walls, comfy green banquettes, shiny woods and perfectly placed flowers. This popular and unpretentious Japanese restaurant is a celebration of soba (pure buckwheat) noodles which are prepared to perfection. Settle in with tasting plates of pickled vegetables, prawn tempura with soba noodles, tori dango (fried ground-chicken meatballs with Japanese herbs), or soba gaku (small prawns rolled with soba and shiso leaf). Do sample the seiro soba—cold buckwheat noodles presented on a lacquered tray with a superb dipping sauce called dashi. There's even a dessert soba dumpling in a sweet red bean soup, or vanilla ice cream with red bean topping. Service is friendly and very helpful. Closed Monday. $$$ 🍷🍷🍷

★★★½ **JEAN-CLAUDE**—137 Sullivan Street (near Prince Street)—475-9232—Nowhere outside of Montparnasse will you find a restaurant with as much quirky charm as Jean-Claude. Pass by the owner's motorcycle prominently displayed outside the brick facade, through a crowded, smoky bar with a buttercream interior. You're greeted by a mix of jazz and rock music; a place people drop into at all hours—in fact, the later you go, the more fun you'll have. Dress down. Ravioli with peas and leeks, grilled mackerel, roasted salmon with spinach, lamb with potato gratin, sweetbreads with mesclun, luscious crème brûlée. No credit cards. No reservations. Closed Monday. $$½ 🍷

★★½ **JERRY'S**—101 Prince Street (between Mercer and Greene Streets)—966-9464—The decor is updated diner, and the ambience very relaxed. But the kitchen is anything but laid back in its diligent preparation of American specialties. Duck breast and duck sausage salad, spinach salad with Swedish bacon, Cobb salad, grilled swordfish with cucumber tomato raita, and wholesome sandwiches. Excellent frites. $$½ 🍷🍷

★★½ **JOUR ET NUIT**—227 West Broadway (at Grand Street)—925-5971—The chic Gallic impudence that once characterized this place, with the worthies seated upstairs, the *plucs* downstairs, diminished as the novelty effect of the space wore off, and now it's less unnerving to dine here. They do a good, solid job with bistro classics, though the menu's nothing remarkable. Potato chèvre, onglet (hanger steak), leg of lamb, grilled salmon, crème brûlée. $$$ 🍷🍷

★★ **THE KITCHEN CLUB**—30 Prince Street (near Mott Street)—274-0025—Teal velvet draperies part and you enter an eclectic and somewhat rarefied oasis tucked away in Little Italy. Kitschy tables set with lacquered chopsticks, amethyst votive candles, and a collection of photos, mirrors and an infusion of incense set the stage. Chef/owner Marja Samsom's menu is unconventional yet satisfying. Splendid chicken soup, black trumpet mushrooms, fricassee of soba noodles in broth, bento-style "box" dinner with stuffed quail, milk-fed veal, baby lamb chops, grilled duck sausage, apple tart, linzertorte. Closed Monday. $$$ 🍷🍷

★★★ **LE PESCADOU**—18 King Street (corner of Avenue of the Americas)—924-3434—You are welcomed with humor and charm into a cozy, glowing space with brick and sponged walls, pleasing murals and sidewalk dining in season. Le Pescadou, as the name suggests, specializes in seafood with a Provençal accent. Although the menu is limited, the kitchen delivers good, honest fare prepared with the freshest ingredients. Salmon tartare with lime-marinated scallops, socca tarte, shrimp sautéed with chili oil, grilled halibut, salmon with horseradish crust, bouillabaisse, fruit tarts, chocolate mousse cake. $$$½ 🍷🍷

★★ **LUCKY STRIKE**—59 Grand Street (between West Broadway and Wooster)—941-0479—This is a dark, crowded and noisy bistro with cramped seating that truly comes alive at night. Raw woods, mirrors and brass railings give it great character. Service is harried, but no one seems to care. Crab cakes with cucumber salad, steamed mussels with tomatoes and wine sauce, grilled polenta with wild mushrooms, steak frites, grilled lamb chops with roasted potatoes, ricotta ravioli with butter and sage, bread pudding, crème caramel, chocolate cake. $$$ 🍷🍷

★★½ **MATCH**—160 Mercer Street (between Prince and Houston)—343-0020—A hot dining scene with brick walls, green banquettes, and distressed wood, which actually boasts some serious food—although if you are not known, dinner reservations can be problematic. (Alternatively, Match is a good spot for a SoHo lunch.) Potato chive dumplings with onion marmalade, spring rolls, fried blue corn ravioli, tunaburger with wasabi pickle salad, duck pizza with shiitake mushrooms, grilled salmon in ginger scallion broth, Match cheesecake. $$$½ 🍷

★★½ **OMEN RESTAURANT**—113 Thompson Street (between Prince and Spring Streets)—925-8923—This casual and inviting country-style Japanese restaurant boasts an original and well executed menu. An effective use of wood paneling creates a serene atmosphere. You'll find traditional dishes like tuna sashimi and mixed tempura, along with innovative preparations such as tuna with mountain yam and quail egg, salmon sautéed in saké, and scallops with peanut cream. Try the house saké. $$$ 🍷

★★ **PENANG**—109 Spring Street (near Mercer Street)—274-8883—New York is not exactly rife with Malaysian restaurants, but this is a worthwhile effort, replete with a tropical rain forest look. The waiters and waitresses are dressed in Malaysian garb, and everybody raves about the peanut pancake. But some of the food here is inconsistent, and while other dishes are very tasty, they can lack finesse. Beef rendang, Penang noodles, pork spareribs. $$½ 🍷

★★ **PRAVDA**—281 Lafayette Street (between Prince and Houston Streets)—2226-4944—On looks alone, this place deserves a visit—that is, provided you pass muster with the bouncers and traverse the velvet rope. A cavernous and smoky spot (cigars and cigarettes are welcome) resembling a Russian avant-garde stage set from the 1930s, it attracts a black-clad crowd that looks like it was hand-picked by central casting. Tables are available on a reservation-only basis, so the bar is always packed. You peruse a menu of some 75 different vodkas, complemented by Russian and domestic caviar, along with teasers like Pravda potato chips, spinach and cheese pirozhki, roasted eggplant caviar, a surprisingly good borscht. $$→$$$$$ 🍷🍷

★★★½ **PROVENCE**—38 MacDougal Street (near Prince Street)—475-7500—This charming and airy bistro, owned by the dedicated Jean family, is complemented by one of the city's most enchanting gardens replete with a working fountain and handsome green latticework. Dining here on authentic Provençal fare, you truly experience the sensation of getting away from it all. Moules gratinées, pissaladière, homemade pâtés, soupe de poissons, fresh cod with tapenade and tomato, braised rabbit with olives, steak (with exceptional) frites, crème brûlée Catalan, marquise au chocolat. Amex only. $$$ 🍷🍷🍷

★★★½ **QUILTY'S**—177 Prince Street (near Sullivan Street)—254-1260—Two small and sparse rooms done up in white and gray create a clean and crisp effect, offset by glowing sconces. The mounted butterflies may tip you off to the restaurant's moniker; Quilty is a character in lepidopterist-author Vladimir Nabokov's "Lolita." Chef Katy Spark's food is well-balanced and full of textural contrasts. Tuna tartare with sevruga and sake-cured lemons, almond-fried squid, grilled pork tenderloin wrapped in pancetta with cumin-roasted apples, peppered yellowfin tuna with papaya ginger, berry and mango gratin with hazelnut praline, apple tart for two, tangerine pots de crème. $$$½ 🍷🍷🍷

★★ **RAOUL'S**—180 Prince Street (at Sullivan Street)—966-3518—One of New York's most atmospheric French bistros. The menu is full of traditional offerings such as leeks vinaigrette, steak au poivre, grilled salmon, profiteroles—all nicely executed, but without tremendous flair. Recently renovated. $$$$ 🍷🍷

★★★½ **SANZIN**—180 Spring Street (at Thompson Street)—965-0710—Another bit of Paris descends on SoHo. Behind the terra cotta facade is this ultra-smart bistro with clean lines, a surrealist-inspired mural, a crowded and smoky bar room and an intimate space in back. Chef Johannes Sanzin (he trained in Paris, then at Bouley and Le Bernardin) has a magical touch with infusions and seasonings and a particular strength with fish and seafood. His menu is compact but varied, as is the wine list. Service is spunky but slow. Seared thyme-crusted tuna with marinated fennel, grilled shrimp in tomato-coriander vinaigrette, pan-roasted skate dusted with walnuts, roasted Cornish hen with Thai basil jus, braised lamb shank, red pear pudding, apple tart with walnut mousse. $$$½ 🍷🍷

★★★ **SAVORE**—200 Spring Street (corner of Sullivan Street)—431-1212—Savore's owner Paolo Alavina looks to Renaissance Florence for inspiration. The interior is clean and simple, as in the best Florentine trattorias, but the food has color and taste. Chef Patrizio Siddu turns every dish into a burst of flavor, and his bountiful Tuscan seafood stew called cacciuco is a classic rendering. In spring and summer, people vie for the window tables in this truly charming corner setting in SoHo. Pappa al pomodoro, insalata di Medici, spaghetti with ricotta topped by orange and lemon, pappardelle with wild boar, lamb chops, panna cotta, chocolate torta. $$$ 🍷🍷

★★★½ **SAVOY**—70 Prince Street (near Crosby)—219-8570—We prefer the intimate downstairs space with its warm, honey-hued glow, paper lanterns, metallic gold-screened ceiling and walls dotted with patterned plates—truly one of SoHo's coziest spots. The new upstairs dining room is a total contrast in its contemporary design, with a constantly-changing $48 fixed price menu. But no matter where you sit, you are sure to enjoy Savoy's esoteric cuisine, which focuses on market ingredients. Chick pea purée with garlic croutons, tomato soup with mushroom and bacon, tuna with lentils, fettucine with duck and cabbage, sautéed cod with artichoke crostini, calf's liver with fried endives and caper topped with mustard sauce, apple pecan cake with vanilla ice cream, spiced prune cake with caramel cider sauce, chocolate pot de crème with cherry shortbread. $$$½ 🍷🍷🍷

★★½ **SOHO KITCHEN AND BAR**—103 Greene Street (near Prince Street)—925-1866—Enormous brick dining room serving good pizzas, pastas, and simple grilled fare. But the real draw is more than 100 wines available by the glass and 21 extraordinary taster's "flights" of eight wines each, poured in 1.5 ounce servings, which range from French country wines to international chardonnays and Chilean cabernet sauvignons. Clearly NYC's best wine bar. $$½ 🍷🍷🍷🍷

★★ **SOHO STEAK**—90 Thompson Street (between Prince and Spring Streets)—226-0602—Jean-Claude Iacovelli's (he also owns Jean-Claude and Café Lure) latest outpost is a mecca for good value. It's a small and unassuming space with a carved-wood bar, paper-topped tables and walls lined with vintage photos and bottles of young wine. The staff is dressed in civilian garb, which can lead to confusion, but service is prompt nonetheless. The quality of beef may be uneven, but with steak au poivre going for $12, it's worth the gamble. Beef tartare with crisped capers, grilled foie gras, braised oxtail ravioli, steak frites, double-cut pork chop with organic barley, herb-braised cod with broccoli rabe, crème brûlée, cold melon soup. Interesting selection of petit château wines. $$½ 🍷🍷

★★★ **SWEET OPHELIA'S**—430 Broome Street (at Crosby Street)—343-8000—Escape into this intimate and dimly-lit dining room packed with personality. Its deep-red lacquered walls, primitive paintings, dark woods and flickering candles transport you far away from the city. The mood is casual and easy; the service is friendly and relaxed. Billing itself as an "Upsouth restaurant and lounge," there is live jazz on Wednesdays and weekends. Every night, you can dine on delectable hushpuppies, deviled crab cakes, fried okra, sweet potato ravioli with shrimp, barbecue ribs, Southern fried chicken, banana pudding pie, blueberry cobbler. $$$ 🍷

★★★½ **ZOË**—90 Prince Street (corner of Mercer Street)—966-6722—Thalia and Stephen Loffredo's dynamic restaurant, with soaring terra cotta-columns, sleek marble tabletops and an ample sprinkling of hand-blown glass remains a top SoHo destination (reserve well in advance for weekend meals). The kitchen is now presided over by chef Kevin Reilly, whose menu is marginally less eclectic than his predecessor's, and the all-American wine list continues to shine. The fare is fundamentally American, with Mediterranean and Pacific rim borrowings. Ricotta and roasted garlic gnocchi, grilled quail and mango jam, house-smoked salmon and manchengo cheese sandwich. Grilled chicken with noodle cake, boneless pork loin with smoked ham hocks, roasted salmon with mashed potatoes, warm apple crisp, chocolate crème brûlée, brown butter pear cake. $$$$ 🍷🍷🍷🍷

LITTLE ITALY, CHINATOWN, LOWER EAST SIDE

★★ **ANGELO'S**—146 Mulberry Street (near Grand Street)—966-1277—A very old-fashioned Italian-American spot (opened in 1902) and certainly better than most of the tourist haunts that surround it. This place has a homey feel, with its simple decor and black-and-white tile floors, and is as good as you'll find in the neighborhood. Go with the whole family. Pappardelle with a vegetable sauce, orrechiette with broccoli di rabe. Closed Monday. $$$ 🍷🍷

★★½ **CANTON**—45 Division Street (near Market Street)—226-4441—You don't come here for the decor, which is cheerful but unassuming. Instead, traditional Cantonese fare prepared with the freshest ingredients makes this a worthwhile trek. Service is friendly and accommodating. The concise menu is supplemented daily by fish and seafood specials. Mushroom egg drop soup, spring roll, dim sum, stuffed clams, ginger scallion noodles, crispy boneless chicken, jumbo shrimp with Canton sauce, crispy boneless chicken, scallion pork loin. Dinner reservations are essential. No credit cards. $$$ 🍷

★★ **FERRARA**—195 Grand Street (at Mulberry Street)—226-6150—If you wish to get a good aroma of what Little Italy is all about, walk into Ferrara and get a whiff of the freshly brewed espresso and cappuccino, then sit at one of the little tables and have yourself a cannoli—a crisp pastry filled with cream—or a sfogliatelle, flakey pastry with a custard-like cream. This is an authentic Southern Italian café. $

★★½ **IL CORTILE**—125 Mulberry Street (near Hester Street)—226-6060—More elegant than most ristorante in Little Italy, this multiroomed space boasts an ancient Roman brick wall, a garden room with a skylight, and lovely tables by the window. It draws a fair share of celebs (actor Danny DeVito actually got married here), and the food is somewhat more imaginative than you'll find elsewhere in the neighborhood. Shrimp with mozzarella, prosciutto, and pignoli, veal in robust Barolo wine sauce, macadamia nut cake. $$$$ 🍷🍷

★★ **KATZ'S DELICATESSEN**—205 East Houston Street (near Orchard Street)—254-2246—If you want to get to know what a real NYC deli is like, this is your place—a longstanding favorite of New Yorkers who like to shop for bargains on adjacent Orchard Street and then repair to Katz's for big fat sandwiches of steaming tongue, brisket of beef, and corned beef, garlicky frankfurters, dripping pickles, greasy fries, and a bottle of cream soda, served cafeteria style. You've got to move fast and know what you want, because the counter men can make a sandwich faster than you can say, "pastrami-on-rye." $½

★★ **MANDARIN COURT**—61 Mott Street (near Canal Street)—608-3838—Though the command of English here leaves something to be desired, and the pace can be chaotic at times, this wildly popular dim sum parlor warrants the trip to Chinatown. On a Sunday you will probably wait a few minutes for a table while you watch a parade of wonderfully steamy dim sum in all shapes pass you by. The food is cheap, the dim sum fresh, and everybody sits at communal tables. No wine list. $

★★ **NOODLE TOWN**—28½ Bowery (near Canal Street)—349-0923—The name is not encouraging and the place is not much to look at, but this Chinatown noodle parlor serves up fabulous Hong Kong style fare at very low prices ($8.50 for a half duck is the top price on the menu). Don't miss the wide Hong Kong noodles with beef, the duck and dumpling soup, or the pan-fried noodles with black beans. No credit cards. $$

★★½ **SPQR**—133 Mulberry Street (near Broome Street)—925-3120—Easily the most lavish restaurant in the neighborhood, with marvelous brickwork, romantic lighting, and an extensive menu, SPQR (the Latin abbreviation for "the Senate and the People of Rome") is a good place to go with a large group or to hold a party. Tony Bennett actually does drop by now and then for the scaloppine SPQR with prosciutto, spinach, zucchini, mozzarella, and a sherry wine sauce. Also good is the zuppe di pesce marinara, the fettuccine with mascarpone cheese and sun-dried tomatoes, and the massive double-cut veal chop. One of the area's best wine lists. $$$½ 🍷🍷🍷

GREENWICH VILLAGE (EAST)

★★★ ACME BAR & GRILL—9 Great Jones Street (near Broadway)—420-1934—We are delighted to find some of the best Southern cooking we've ever eaten being made in the Village. The place looks like a roadside eatery off Route 66—brick walls, rickety furniture, plenty of neon beer signs and scores of hot sauces lining the walls—your waiter will advise you on their particular characteristics the way a sommelier will a wine. Owners Chandler Sante, Don Rothschild and Sharon Barnard took a good look at what makes Southern food so savory and use better ingredients than most of their Southern counterparts. What's more, Acme has its own microbrewery that makes a good American pale ale, as well as 20 other bottled beers. Crabcakes, hush puppies, fried shrimp, fried chicken, country ham with red-eye gravy, pecan pie. $$½ 🍷

★★★ COL LEGNO—231 East 9th Street near Third Avenue)—777-4650—A sparse and unassuming trattoria, such as one might find in Tuscany, with a very capable kitchen. White beans with sage and garlic, roasted potatoes with thyme and parmesan cheese, pappa al pomodoro. There are five excellent pizzas prepared in a brick oven including standards like the Margherita and less conventional combinations like anchovies, capers, tomato sauce, and garlic. Tagliatelle with leek, tomato, and rosemary sauce, spinach lasagna with ricotta, truffle scented quail with grilled polenta, pork chops with fennel oil, tiramisù. $$½ 🍷🍷

★★★★ ENNIO & MICHAEL—539 LaGuardia Place (near Bleecker Street)—677-8577—Two indefatigable Abruzzese owners run this charming, sprightly Village place serving robust and zesty Italian food at a fair

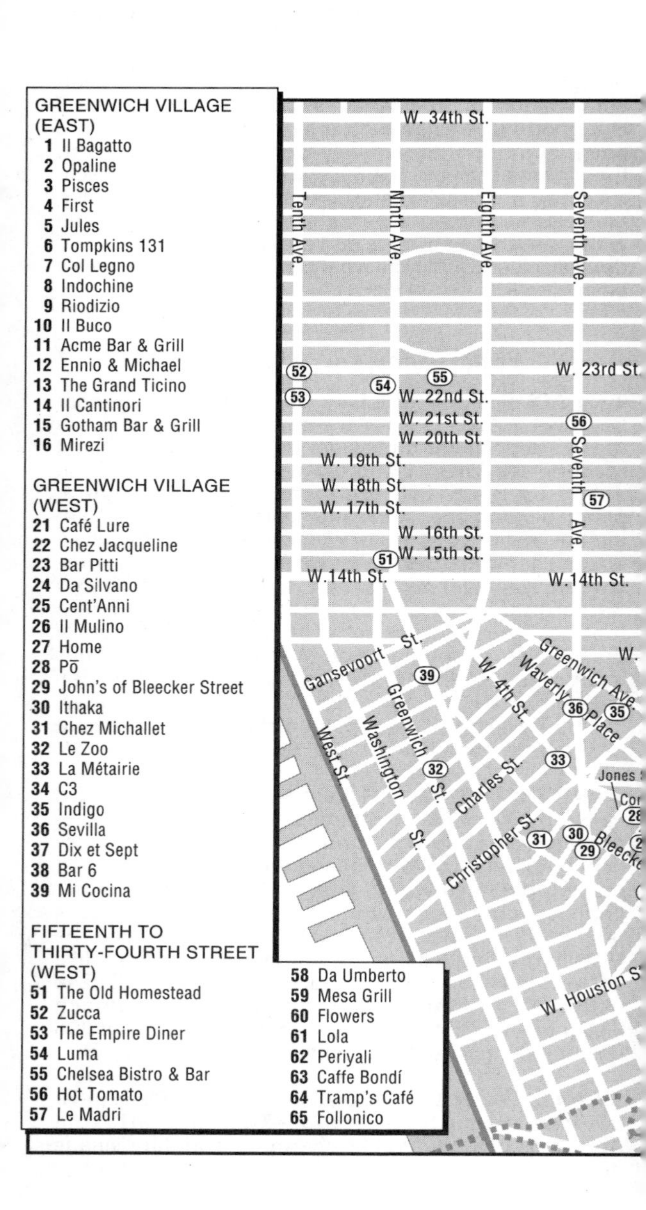
GREENWICH VILLAGE (EAST)
1 Il Bagatto
2 Opaline
3 Pisces
4 First
5 Jules
6 Tompkins 131
7 Col Legno
8 Indochine
9 Riodizio
10 Il Buco
11 Acme Bar & Grill
12 Ennio & Michael
13 The Grand Ticino
14 Il Cantinori
15 Gotham Bar & Grill
16 Mirezi
GREENWICH VILLAGE (WEST)
21 Café Lure
22 Chez Jacqueline
23 Bar Pitti
24 Da Silvano
25 Cent'Anni
26 Il Mulino
27 Home
28 Pō
29 John's of Bleecker Street
30 Ithaka
31 Chez Michallet
32 Le Zoo
33 La Métairie
34 C3
35 Indigo
36 Sevilla
37 Dix et Sept
38 Bar 6
39 Mi Cocina
FIFTEENTH TO THIRTY-FOURTH STREET (WEST)
51 The Old Homestead
52 Zucca
53 The Empire Diner
54 Luma
55 Chelsea Bistro & Bar
56 Hot Tomato
57 Le Madri
58 Da Umberto
59 Mesa Grill
60 Flowers
61 Lola
62 Periyali
63 Caffe Bondí
64 Tramp's Café
65 Follonico
W. 34th St.
Tenth Ave.
Ninth Ave.
Eighth Ave.
Seventh Ave.
W. 23rd St.
W. 22nd St.
W. 21st St.
W. 20th St.
W. 19th St.
W. 18th St.
W. 17th St.
W. 16th St.
W. 15th St.
W.14th St.
W.14th St.
Seventh Ave.
Gansevoort St.
Greenwich Ave.
Waverly Place
W. 4th St.
West St.
Washington St.
Greenwich St.
Charles St.
Christopher St.
Jones
W. Houston St.

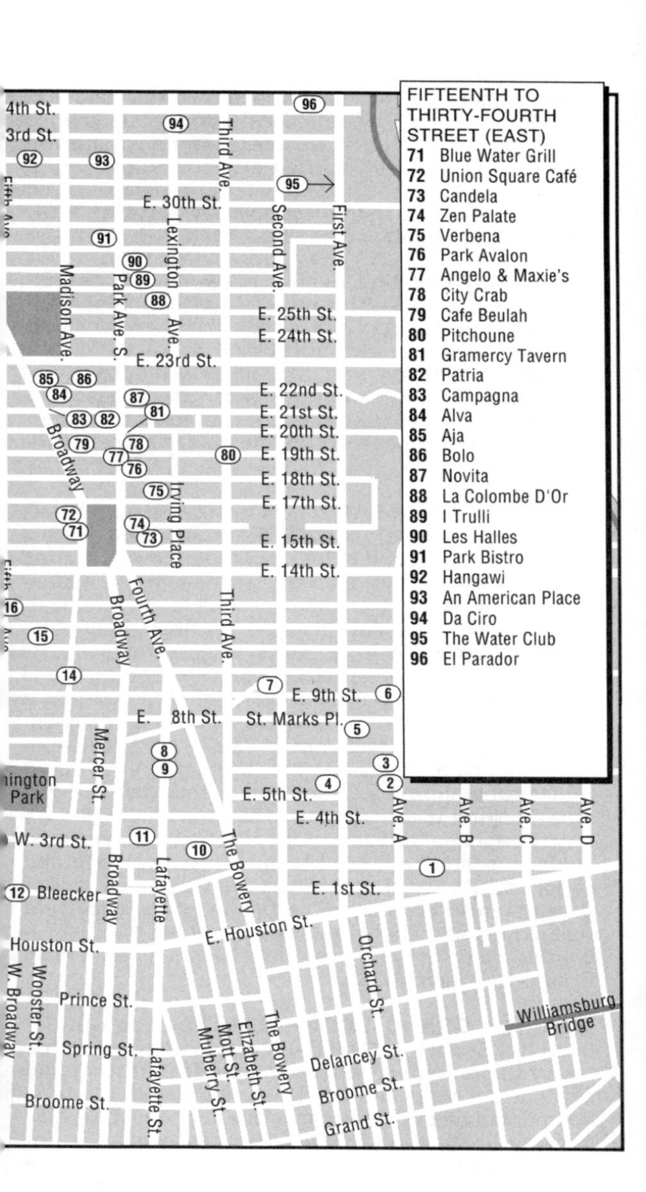
FIFTEENTH TO THIRTY-FOURTH STREET (EAST)
71 Blue Water Grill
72 Union Square Café
73 Candela
74 Zen Palate
75 Verbena
76 Park Avalon
77 Angelo & Maxie's
78 City Crab
79 Cafe Beulah
80 Pitchoune
81 Gramercy Tavern
82 Patria
83 Campagna
84 Alva
85 Aja
86 Bolo
87 Novita
88 La Colombe D'Or
89 I Trulli
90 Les Halles
91 Park Bistro
92 Hangawi
93 An American Place
94 Da Ciro
95 The Water Club
96 El Parador
3rd St.
Third Ave.
E. 30th St.
Lexington Ave.
Second Ave.
First Ave.
Madison Ave.
Park Ave. S.
E. 25th St.
E. 24th St.
E. 23rd St.
E. 22nd St.
E. 21st St.
E. 20th St.
E. 19th St.
E. 18th St.
E. 17th St.
E. 15th St.
E. 14th St.
Broadway
Irving Place
Fourth Ave.
Mercer St.
E. 9th St.
E. 8th St.
St. Marks Pl.
E. 5th St.
E. 4th St.
Ave. A
Ave. B
Ave. C
Ave. D
W. 3rd St.
Bleecker
Lafayette
The Bowery
E. 1st St.
E. Houston St.
Houston St.
Orchard St.
Wooster St.
W. Broadway
Prince St.
Spring St.
Lafayette St.
Mulberry St.
Mott St.
Elizabeth St.
Delancey St.
Broome St.
Grand St.
Williamsburg Bridge

price. Definitely one of downtown's best Italian restaurants proffering a vestige of what the Village used to be like decades ago. The set-back outdoor patio is absolutely delightful in good weather. Order anything with garlic. Zucchini fritti, stuffed artichokes, gnocchi in tomato and basil, roasted baby lamb, wholewheat linguine with clams, cannoli, strawberry sorbetto. Amex only. Closed Monday. $$$½ 🍷🍷

★★½ **FIRST**—87 First Avenue (between 5th and 6th Streets)—674-3823—This metal-sheathed interior with a popular bar sets an amusing, upbeat tone for Sam DeMarco's menu. The portions are bountiful, and because the lighting is so dim, the presentation is next to impossible to discern. Crabcakes, goat cheese quesadilla, double-thick pork chop, rotisserie free range chicken, warm chocolate pudding cake, caramel crème brûlée. $$$ 🍷🍷

★★★★½ **GOTHAM BAR & GRILL**—12 East 12th Street (near Fifth Avenue)—620-4020—Chef Alfred Portale has become a legend in his own time. He has exerted tremendous influence on chefs and restaurants nationwide for his culinary creativity, presentation and overall dedication to quality. But time has finally caught up with this cavernous trailblazer of a restaurant, with its draped ceiling fixtures, stone pillars and teal trim. It is dimly lit, noisy and too crowded for its own good. As a result, service is harried, indifferent and a tad mechanical. Yet the cuisine itself remains stellar, with its whimsical mile-high presentations. Goat cheese ravioli in minestrone, smoked salmon on potato galette, wild game terrine with haricots verts, monkfish tail with Savoy cabbage, grilled saddle of rabbit with steamed spinach, seared yellowfin tuna with pappardelle and caponata. Pastry chef Wonyee Tom's artful array of desserts include caramelized banana cake, chocolate malt coupe and Valrhona chocolate bread pudding. A worthy wine list with good bets by the glass. $19.96 fixed price lunch. $$$$$ 🍷🍷🍷🍷

★★½ **THE GRAND TICINO**—228 Thompson Street (near 3rd Street)—777-5922—A very cozy place with a real Village feeling, where scenes from the movie Moonstruck were filmed. The basic Italian menu is augmented by good daily specials, and the antipasti is the way to stave off hunger. The service staff is not always on its toes, and the wine list could use some upgrading. Ravioli with walnut cream, penne all'arrabiata, chicken with eggplant and sun-dried tomatoes, calf's liver Venetian style. $$$½ 🍷

★★ **IL BAGATTO**—192 East 2nd Street (between Avenues A and B)—228-0977—This is a tiny, boisterous and hip place with brick walls, candle light and blaring music. But the tables are often over-booked and the wait at the downstairs bar (with its antiseptic smell) resembles purgatory. Yet Bagatto's minuscule kitchen, slightly larger than a toll booth, produces some of the most heavenly pasta at the lowest prices in town (around $8.00). Entrees are in the same bracket, so it is impossible to spend much of your money on food; top price on the wine list is only $31, with many listings around $20. Antipasti, fennel and mushroom salad, salad Caprese, gnocchetti verdi with gorgonzola sauce, penne all'arrabiata, spaghetti with spicy tomato sauce and pancetta, panna cotta with berry sauce, ricotta cheesecake. $$ 🍷

★★½ **IL BUCO**—47 Bond Street (between Lafayette and Bowery)—533-1932—An antique shop by day, at night this space takes on the persona of a restaurant. The setting is as eclectic as the cuisine: antiques galore, vintage toy cars, refectory tables, ceiling fans, lanterns and plenty of candles. This is a fun, relaxed and easy-going spot, but seating can be cramped and the staff can be harried. Graze the menu and share your selections. Bruschetta di Pomodoro, grilled baby calamari with fresh tomato, roasted rabbit salad with shaved fennel and herbs, saffron risotto cakes with sautéed wild mushrooms, gambas in sea salt. Ricotta cheese cake, hazelnut pudding with chocolate frosting. No credit cards. Closed Monday. $$$½ 🍷🍷🍷

★★★½ **IL CANTINORI**—32 East 10th Street (near University Place)—673-6044—With its stuccoed walls and dramatic floral displays, this rustic trattoria remains a comforting and atmospheric destination for solid Tuscan fare. The kitchen produces enticing pasta specials, along with satisfying dishes like grilled baby octopus with capers, tuna carpaccio, bean and spinach soup, calf's liver with sage, roasted monkfish with rosemary, sautéed salmon with fennel. Superb semifreddo. $$$½ 🍷🍷🍷

★★ **INDOCHINE**—430 Lafayette Street (near Astor

Place)—505-5111—For some time, this was a true destination restaurant, drawing diners from all around town, as well as the crowd from the Public Theater across the street. It is now far less of a scene, but remains a worthwhile addition to the neighborhood. Sweet and sour shrimp soup, fried spring rolls with fresh crab meat, Vietnamese ravioli with chicken and shiitake mushrooms, crispy whole red snapper, sliced filet of beef. $$$ 🍷🍷

★★ **JULES**—65 St. Mark's Place (near First Avenue)—477-5560—A very authentic and amiable Montparnasse-style bistro, which comes complete with a grungy left-bank look and period posters. Although portions are extremely generous, the food lacks finesse, and the kitchen would be wise to favor flavor over volume. Vegetable terrine with goat cheese, moules marinières, gambas Provençal, steak frites, mushroom ravioli, Grand Marnier mousse. $$½ 🍷🍷🍷

★★★ **MIREZI**—59 Fifth Avenue (near 13th Street)—242-9709—Mirezi is as sleek as a lacquered chopstick. This long narrow space—with its yellow-sponged walls, mini video monitors, bullseye upholstery in taupe and Burgundy, and candle-lit copper-topped tables—is clearly a design statement. Service is easy-going and well-informed, and the wine list is exciting and varied. Anita Lo's inspired Korean food is artfully presented on attractive squared plates. Grilled eggplant maki roll, crispy calamari with spicy tomato and coriander sauces, pan-fried mandu dumplings, wok-fried seafood and rice noodles with garlic chives, grilled filet of salmon with black ginger butter, pan-roasted chicken in green curry, poached pear with frangipane and star anise, warm apple sesame tart with green coconut ice cream. $17.50 fixed price lunch. $$$$ 🍷🍷🍷🍷

★★★ **OPALINE**—85 Avenue A (between 5th and 6th Streets)—475-5050—Owners Nicholas Neubauer and Arthur Tullman have taken a large, subterranean space with two tiers, put in a big bar and kept the lighting low. The atmosphere is a little severe but highly spirited, appropriate for a place whose name refers to the addictive liqueur also known as absinthe. Chef Edward A. Coleman, lately of Alison on Dominick, has an exceptional talent for modern bistro-style food and serves some of the best French fried potatoes this side of Brussels. Brandade gratinée, mussels steamed in a garlic broth, braised lamb shank with roasted garlic whipped potatoes, sautéed monkfish with braised vegetables and brown butter, herb-roasted chicken, fruit clafoutis. $$$ 🍷🍷

★★½ **PISCES**—95 Avenue A (at 6th Street)—260-6660—This long and casual space is accessorized with a wooden ship's model and a bright neon sign proclaiming "shrimp." As its name suggests, seafood and fresh fish are the focal point of this popular restaurant, but the food is much more elaborate and appealing than the decor would suggest, evidenced by the packed reservation book. Tuna seviche, cod cakes with fennel salad, phyllo-fried shrimp, mesquite-smoked trout, penne with cured salmon, cappuccino crème caramel, berry and lemon tart, strawberry rhubarb shortcake. $$½ 🍷🍷

★★½ **RIODIZIO**—417 Lafayette Street (between Astor and 4th Streets)—529-1313—Be prepared for big bang decibels, primary-color banquettes and murals, imposing columns and lampshade-like ceiling fixtures that look like they came from "Rochester Big & Tall." This is a lively and relaxed spot with an equally laid-back service staff and an open kitchen that delivers enormous portions of Brazilian fare. Authentic starters include "Rio Wraps," such as shrimp with bean purée, sweet potato cakes with cabrales cheese, crispy potato teardrops with chicken. Best value for big appetites is the Rodizio, an all-you-can-eat rotisserie of chicken, sausage, beef, ribs and so on, all for $24. Alternatively, consider shrimp and mussels in coconut lime sauce, roasted chicken with mashed sweet potatoes, caramelized banana bread pudding, and naturally, the Carmen Miranda, a cookie hat piled high with sorbets and fruits. $$$ 🍷

★★ **TOMPKINS 131**—131 Avenue A (between 8th and 9th Streets)—777-5642—A simple brick-walled space with a small bar and undulating banquettes, the restaurant features hefty portions and friendly service. It all adds up to a winning formula. There's even good music. The menu is basic American bistro—tuna tartare with cucumber salad, crabcakes with red pepper vinaigrette, grilled portobello salad, grilled duck breast with sweet potato purée, herbed-marinated pork tenderloin with plantain mash, crème brûlée, coconut flan, flourless chocolate cake. $$$ 🍷

GREENWICH VILLAGE (WEST)

★★½ **BAR 6**—502 Avenue of the Americas (between 12th and 13th Streets)—645-2439—In its latest manifestation, this space has been transformed into a low key, but hip bistro (it stays open until 4:00 AM) with a Moroccan accent. It looks a bit like a stage set, but the kitchen clearly works. Tapenade, hummus and white bean dip with pita bread, grilled calamari, grilled merguez sausages, steak frites, vegetable cous cous, grilled vegetable sandwich, grilled spicy shrimp, sautéed tilapia. $$½ 🍷🍷

★★★½ **BAR PITTI**—268 Sixth Avenue (near Bleecker Street)—982-3300—This rosy interior with sepia-toned prints of Florence conjures up the image of a tiny Tuscan trattoria. You bask in the aromas from the nearby kitchen as you wait for a table (reservations are only accepted for parties of four or more.) The two dining rooms are cramped but convivial, and service is rather home-style. The menu, which emphasizes market-fresh ingredients, includes antipasti, carpaccio, panzanella, delicious taglierini with artichokes, ravioli with spinach and ricotta, osso buco, panna cotta, tartuffo, tiramisù. No credit cards. $$$ 🍷🍷

★★½ **C3**—103 Waverly Place (at MacDougal Street in the Washington Hotel)—254-1200—The subterranean space is a fine example of Greenwich Village style, with its red walls, bare wood floors, low ceilings and oversized paintings of flowers. A new chef, Ted Siegel, has considerably raised the culinary stakes here, for the most part successfully. The waitstaff, by contrast, could be more attentive. Roasted tomato with star anise sauce, poached pear with fennel and frisée, semolina dumplings with wild mushrooms, zinfandel-braised lamb shanks, brownie with vanilla ice cream, banana tart with chocolate ice cream. $$½ 🍷🍷

★★½ **CAFÉ LURE**—169 Sullivan Street (between Bleecker and Houston Streets)—473-2642—Jean-Claude Iacovelli's venture displays many of the characteristic devices of the flagship Jean-Claude (q.v.)—vintage signs and photos, cane chairs, loud music and an attractive, young crowd. The seafood here is largely a success, and very competitively priced. Lobster consommé with spicy shrimp wontons, grilled sardines, sautéed squid with curry, shellfish fricassée, pan seared monkfish with back olive potato purée. $$½ 🍷🍷

★★½ **CENT'ANNI**—50 Carmine Street (near Bleecker Street)—989-9494—A very lively, casual, family-style trattoria nestled in the heart of the Village, which attracts diners from all over the city. Sautéed fava beans, grilled porcini mushrooms, baby roast pheasant, pasta specials such as tortellini with prosciutto and peas in a cream sauce, penne with sun-dried tomatoes, fettucine with rabbit, roasted peppers with anchovies, calamari, veal chop. Sunday dinner can be subdued. $$$ 🍷🍷🍷

★★½ **CHEZ JACQUELINE**—72 MacDougal (between Houston and Bleecker Streets)—505-0727—This is surely one of the most convivial Village bistros—everyone seems to know one another—with warm peach walls, very friendly service, and a competent kitchen. Escargots in a tomato sauce with pastis, frisée with roasted pine nuts and goat cheese, seafood casserole in a light tomato sauce with potatoes, filet mignon with green peppercorn sauce, roasted free range baby chicken with rosemary, apple tart. $$$ 🍷🍷🍷

★★½ **CHEZ MICHALLET**—90 Bedford Street (near Grove Street)—242-8309—Convenient to several Village theaters, this cozy, diminutive bistro proffers an eclectic repertoire. Snails with garlic butter, ravioli of wild mushrooms with truffle broth, grilled garlic sausage with string beans, salmon with mushroom ragoût, Moroccan grilled chicken, magret de canard, Louisiana crayfish, tarte Tatin, profiteroles. $$$ 🍷🍷

★★★ **DA SILVANO**—260 Avenue of the Americas (near Bleecker Street)—982-2343—For years, Da Silvano has quietly gone about its business of serving top-notch, authentic, Italian rustic cooking in an attractive, exposed-brick interior—a formula which has been widely copied around town. As informal as any trattoria in Milan, it draws a loyal crowd. Go with the day's specials, but don't expect any bargains. Crostini, truffled frittata, cod purée, tortellini with bacon, spaghetti alla puttanesca, roasted quail, bistecca alla fiorentina, panna cotta, sorbets. Amex only. $$$$½ 🍷🍷🍷

★★ **DIX ET SEPT**—181 West 10th Street (at the corner of Seventh Avenue and Tenth Street)—645-8023—You step down a flight of stairs to access this sparse and informal space with a traditional menu that is redolent of numerous Paris bistros. (You'll even catch the waft of the occasional Gitane at the bar.) Snails in garlic butter, onion soup, duck liver mousse, cassoulet, beef bourguignon, breast of duck with thyme honey, chestnut pudding, fresh pear and dried apple crisp, bittersweet chocolate cake. $$$ 🍷🍷

★★½ **HOME**—20 Cornelia Street (near Bleecker Street)—243-9579—A long, narrow, close space that displays considerable charm. The menu is as homey as the whitewashed decor and wooden banquettes. Oyster Po' boy sandwich, grilled chicken sausage with chick pea stew, grilled guinea hen with yellow-eyed peas, cumin-crusted pork chops, chocolate pudding. Home is a soothing spot for a weekend brunch (with alfresco dining in season). No credit cards. $$½ 🍷🍷

★★★★ **IL MULINO**—86 West 3rd Street (between Sullivan and Thompson Streets)—673-3783—From the moment you arrive at this comfortable brick-walled space you feel upbeat. The greeting is friendly, the complimentary antipasti abundant and the service attentive yet discreet. A perfect rose is placed on each table. Green-painted chairs and palm trees complete the look. We particularly enjoy dining here at lunch, when there is no crush at the bar. The menu is traditional Abruzzese—robust, yet artfully prepared—a labor of love from the brothers Gino and Bernardo Maschu. Clams casino (the bacon is home-smoked), superb ravioli with porcini mushrooms and black truffles, rolled veal braised in white wine and cream with wild mushrooms, chicken with sausage and roasted peppers, filet of beef with spicy caper sauce, cheesecake, strawberries with zabaglione, tiramisù. $$$$ 🍷🍷

★★★ **INDIGO**—142 West 10th Street (between Greenwich and Waverly Place)—691-7757—Talented chef Scott Bryan (he is also executive chef at Luma q.v.) has turned this cozy brick-walled space, which has been home to many restaurant ventures, into a true downtown destination. There is a commodious bar area up front which glows under warm lighting, a simple and larger main salon and friendly service throughout. Bryan's menu is eclectic and inspired. Tuscan white bean soup, wild mushroom strudel, grilled Thai beef salad, sage-roasted chicken with polenta, grilled hangar steak with potato purée, roast leg of lamb with garlic spinach, bitter chocolate torte, berry gratin. $$$½ 🍷🍷

★★ **ITHAKA**—48 Barrow Street (near Seventh Avenue)—727-8886—Crisp white stucco walls and an array of potted plants create a clean and friendly feeling. We prefer the back room with its relaxed, countrified look. Taramosalata (cod roe spread), tzatziki (yogurt-cucumber spread), melitzanosalata (roasted eggplant spread), kalokythakia skordalia (deep fried zucchini), oktapodaki (grilled octopus), saganaki (grilled Greek cheese), garides grecolimano (baked shrimp) youvetski (baked baby lamb), assorted Greek pastry. $$½ 🍷🍷

★★½ **JOHN'S OF BLEECKER STREET**—278 Bleecker Street (near Seventh Avenue)—243-1680—John's makes the best traditional Neapolitan pizzas in New York, with a good crisp crust, neither too thick or too thin, freshly made sauces, good cheese, and a baking process that makes all the difference. This is the Promised Land for great pie. No credit cards. $ 🍷

★★★½ **LA MÉTAIRIE**—189 West 10th Street (corner West 4th Street near Seventh Avenue)—989-0343—This tiny spot presided over by owner Sylvain Fareri brings the charm of the French countryside to the hub of Greenwich Village. The atmosphere is casual but the kitchen is very serious. The Provençal-inspired fare ranks high on any gastronome's list: seafood sausage, garlic mousse, Hudson Valley foie gras, lobster risotto with wild mushrooms, roasted rack of lamb with vegetable tart, seared tuna with quinona and plum wine sauce, coffee crème brûlée, praline cake. $$$½ 🍷🍷🍷🍷

★★★ **LE ZOO**—314 West 11th Street (corner Greenwich Street)—242-9435—A diminutive corner bistro with brick walls, ceiling fans, period posters and terrific music, led by a savvy team of friends who are talented and genuinely charming. The staff is delightful as well. No reservations are accepted at this casual spot, but everyone is treated like an instant regular and the well prepared and appealing menu is worth a wait. (Go before 8:00 PM or after 10:00 PM unless you want to encounter a zoo of a crowd.) Crispy sweetbreads with frisée salad, feuilleté of bay scallops and leeks, goat cheese terrine, sautéed skate with mustard sauce, free-range chicken with honey and spices, braised cod with mushroom crust, coffee crème brûlée, warm chocolate cake. A succinct but solid wine list. $$$ 🍷🍷

★★ **MI COCINA**—57 Jane Street (near Hudson Street)—627-8273—There's nothing clichéd about this delightful Mexican restaurant presided over by the former executive chef of the Cinco de Mayo "chain." The decor is traditional in an understated way—a smattering of colorful tiles and pink-hued walls. Authenticity is the byword: empanitas de picadillo, (turnovers filled with beef and olives), slivers of cornmeal with goat cheese and onions, chicken enchiladas, fajitas, shrimp with chipotle peppers. Excellent margaritas. $$½ 🍷

★★★★ **PŌ**—31 Cornelia Street (near Bleecker Street)—645-2189—A very casual and inviting sliver of a place, with tin ceilings and white wainscoting, presided over by celebrity chef Mario Batali (he hosts a regular program on the Food Network). Pō delivers extremely sophisticated, flavorful and reasonably-priced Northern Italian fare. Sautéed calamari with sun-dried tomatoes, grappa-cured salmon with lemon crostini, white bean ravioli, scavatelli with hot sausage and caramelized parsnips, grilled rabbit sausage with sweet potatoes, roasted monkfish with porcini, fresh strawberries with balsamic vinegar, Pō sundae, comice pears with homemade mascarpone and crushed biscotti. Five course tasting menu $25. $$$ 🍷🍷🍷

★★★ **SEVILLA**—62 Charles Street (near Seventh Avenue)—243-9513—A bustling and spirited Spanish restaurant, heavy on wood paneling and pleasantly informal in nature, catering to a somewhat local crowd. Traditional menu, replete with grilled chorizo, Spanish ham and olives, mariscada with green sauce, paella Valenciana with lobster, is both fresh and deftly prepared. What's more, most entrées fall under the $16 range, making this an excellent spot for diners in search of good fun, good quality, and good value. $$$ 🍷

FIFTEENTH TO THIRTY-FOURTH STREET (EAST)

★★★ **AJA**—937 Broadway (near 22nd Street)—473-8388—This unusual spot, (Aja, by the way, is pronounced like "Asia") looks rather like a student production of "Phantom of the Opera" with its clash of Middle Eastern carpets, Shaker style chairs, stained glass windows, painted plywood panels, exposed air-conditioning ducts, and an enormous chandelier. The noise level is excruciating, and the blaring music makes matters worse. Why bother then? Simple: Chef Gavin Citron's fusion menu, with its tantalizing East-West flavors, rises above the din. Spicy tuna tartare, five-spice grilled squab with caramelized mango, kaffir lime and Thai chilies, grilled rack of lamb rubbed with Indian spices, coconut rice in banana leaves with tropical fruits, peanuts and guajillo syrup. $$$½ 🍷🍷

★★★ **ALVA**—36 East 22nd Street (off Broadway)—228-4399—A sleek, narrow and energetic space done up in basic black and blue, with black-and-white photographs decking the walls, Alva attracts a fashionable crowd. It's owned by Charlie Palmer (Aureole and Lenox Room, q.v.) and presided over by chef Aaron Bashy. Assorted hors d'hoeuvres, Alva Caesar, graavlax with grilled brioche, double-garlic-roasted chicken, pan-seared mahi mahi with vegetable risotto, grilled steak au poivre, Hudson cheesecake, Alva banana ice cream sandwich, Alva chocolate pudding. $$$$ 🍷🍷🍷

★★★★ **AN AMERICAN PLACE**—2 Park Avenue (entrance an 32nd Street)—684-2122—More of an institution than a trend setter, this remains a benchmark destination for American cuisine. It is a also a highly popular spot for a business lunch. The vast, dramatic space is timeless, with multi-colored shard floors and rich paneling. Chef/owner Larry Forgione continues to serve up highly satisfying fare prepared with the freshest ingredients. An American Place Caesar salad, house cured smoked salmon with radish sprout slaw, roasted vidalia onion with shaved pepato cheese and NY State prosciutto, fried Carolina rock shrimp with remoulade dressing and vegetable slaw, crisp soft-shell crab and deviled crab spring roll. Pacific Northwest baby white asparagus and morels with country ham, barbecued free-range chicken burrito, homemade peanut butter ice cream sandwich. $$$$ 🍷🍷🍷

★★½ **ANGELO AND MAXIE'S**—233 Park Avenue South (corner 19th Street)—220-9200—This is "everyman's" steakhouse—without pretension or clubiness, offering good value for well-prepared hearty fare. The cheery and cavernous space looks as if it has been assembled from a kit: mock tin ceilings, reproduction stained glass fixtures and posters, wood paneling and an open kitchen. Nevertheless, the effect is upbeat. Service bustles, but beware the heavy-handed wine pouring. Raw bar selections, graavlax, Caesar salad, chopped steak, filet mignon (14 oz. serving is a steal at $19.00), whole roasted chicken, hot fudge sundae, pecan pie. True to the times, there is a smart-looking cigar bar in back. $$$½ 🍷🍷

★★½ **BLUE WATER GRILL**—31 Union Square West (at 16th Street)—675-9500—This deep and dramatic space was once home to the famed Metropolis Bank. Marble walls and an elaborate ceiling with fine architectural details are the only hints of its heritage. Bold nautically-colored slip covers, vibrant jazz (taped during the day, live in a downstairs dining room at night) and ample seating on two levels give this restaurant a new identity. As the room fills up, noise can be a problem, but the overall experience is fun and relaxed. Bamboo-steamed shrimp dumplings, lobster spring roll, fresh oysters (23 varieties are indexed) Maryland crab cakes, Moroccan-spiced red snapper, pepper-seared tuna, warm Valrhona chocolate cake, cheesecake, hazelnut crème brûlée. $$$ 🍷🍷

★★★½ **BOLO**—23 East 22nd Street (between Park Avenue South and Broadway)—228-2200—Vivid murals incorporating a flamenco dancer, a bullfighter and gyrating spiral graphics contribute to a whimsical atmosphere. Bright contemporary fixtures, tile-work and colorful tableware complete the look. (The room, however, can be noisy.) Executive chef Bobby Flay's menu—Spanish in concept, but clearly American in presentation and execution—is original and festive. Fried squid with anchovy vinaigrette, piquillo peppers filled with salmon tartare, wild mushrooms with goat cheese and chile oil, roasted garlic chicken, horseradish- and potato- crusted red snapper, apple cake with Sherry custard sauce, lemon-raspberry bread pudding, chocolate flan. $$$½ 🍷🍷🍷

★★½ **CAFÉ BEULAH**—39 East 19th Street (between Park Avenue South and Broadway)—777-9700—Vintage photographs, off-white wainscoting, ceiling fans and a checkerboard floor set the stage for a pleasant evocation of Southern style dining. The menu pays homage to such traditional offerings as tomato okra soup, deviled crab cakes, barbecued chicken wings, black eyed pea cakes, shrimp pilau, Alexander's gumbo, Southern fried chicken, collard greens, blueberry cobbler, pecan pie. Appetizers are more successful than the entrees. $$$ 🍷🍷

★★★★ **CAMPAGNA**—24 East 21st Street (between Park Avenue South and Broadway)—460-0900—This glowing trattoria with warm, rustic tones and attractive contemporary artwork is presided over by the energetic chef Mark Straussman, who works the room as assiduously as he rules the kitchen. (He also presides over Fred's in Barneys uptown, q.v.) The staff is professional and polished, and the wine list is rife with vintage Italian estate bottlings. Ravioli with fava beans, old-fashioned eggplant parmigiana, farfalle alla Portofino, roasted halibut with pepper sauce, homemade sausage with broccoli di rabe, herb-smoked squab, bittersweet chocolate mascarpone cake, buttermilk polenta shortcake with blackberry compote. $$$$ 🍷🍷🍷🍷

★★ **CANDELA**—116 East 16th Street (between Irving Place and Union Square East)—254-1600—This vast space resembles a college Rathskeller done up for orientation night. A popular spot with copious candles, loud music and a relaxed and boisterous crowd, it is definitely a 20- to 30-something destination. The menu is highly eclectic, reasonably priced and ambitious. It satisfies just about any craving, but lacks finesse. Risotto cakes with wild mushroom ragoût, fried oysters over spinach with curry, chicken won tons with cilantro dipping sauce, spicy red snapper and rock shrimp cake, fettucine with wild mushrooms au gratin, tuna and white beans ravioli, braised beef short ribs in barolo sauce, grilled shrimp and seared sea scallops, banana beignets, flourless chocolate cake, port roasted pear. $$$ 🍷🍷

★★ **CITY CRAB AND SEAFOOD COMPANY**—235 Park Avenue South (corner of 19th Street)—529-3800—Appropriately, a giant red crab surveys this boisterous space, bedecked with fishy accessories, an inviting bar and oyster station. The downstairs dining room sports high tables and swivel chairs. Upstairs is a tad gloomy, but service throughout is friendly. Try the oyster sampler, popcorn shrimp Cajun style, lobster roll, grilled sea scallops, key lime pie. $$ 🍷🍷

FIFTEENTH TO THIRTY-FOURTH STREET (EAST)

★★★ **DA CIRO**—229 Lexington Avenue (between 33rd and 34th Streets)—532-1636—Tucked away in Murray Hill is this delightful little gem of a trattoria. It sports white stucco walls, green marble tabletops and a wood-burning oven which adds to the comfortable feel. Vintage photographs add personality. Service is attentive, portions are generous, and chef Ciro's cuisine sparkles. Consider the enticing array of casserole appetizers prepared in the wood-burning oven: eggplant with four cheeses, wild mushrooms with arugula and goat cheese, broccoli di rape with sausage. Alternatively, fried calamari, spaghetti boscaliola (with sausage and mushrooms), roasted baby chicken, focaccia robiola, plus a dozen different pizzas. $$$ 🍷🍷

★★ **EL PARADOR**—325 East 34th Street (between First and Second Avenues)—679-6812—For years, Mexican food in Manhattan meant an evening at El Parador. With its stuccoed walls, subdued lighting, and curio-filled bar (that still churns out excellent margaritas), the overall impression is very south of the border, circa 1960. You still dine well, even though the menu is dated. Nachos Royale, chiles rellenos, deep-fried chimichango, taco special, flan, bread pudding. $$½ 🍷

★★★★ **GRAMERCY TAVERN**—42 East 20th Street (near Park Avenue South)—477-0777—The handsome interior with borrowings from post-modern Italy and colonial Massachusetts may send out mixed signals, but there's no confusing chef Tom Colicchio's first-rate American food. Gramercy has all the trademarks of a Danny Meyer restaurant: friendly and efficient service, a superb wine list and good value. Lobster and artichoke salad, marinated hamachi with roast beets, roasted pumpkin soup with sage, white bean raviolini with duck confit, roasted turbot with lemongrass and ginger, spiced squab with licorice root and glazed turnips, sautéed John Dory with fennel confit. There is an enormous cheese selection and inviting desserts such as maple crème brûlée, warm banana tart with caramel ice cream. You can sample the tavern menu in the bar area for considerably less. $$$$½ 🍷🍷🍷🍷

★★★★ **HANGAWI**—12 East 32nd Street (between Fifth and Madison Avenues)—213-0077—A handsome room replete with illuminated wooden screens, a collection of pottery and an array of tea pots. As is customary in traditional Korean restaurants, you remove your shoes upon entering and amble in stocking feet to an elegant, raised seating area, where you perch on a pillow with your legs hanging below. (This requires a modicum of dexterity.) Hangawi's superb vegetarian menu includes pumpkin porridge, vermicelli delight, paper-thin leek pancakes, vegetarian autumn rolls, tofu sandwich, mushrooms galore. Service is subtle and accommodating. Good value. $$$ 🍷

★★★★ **I TRULLI**—122 East 27th Street (between Lexington and Park Avenue South)—481-7372—This convivial trattoria (with a terrific terrace garden for summer dining) gives new meaning to Southern Italian cooking. It has become a true destination, thanks to the originality of its food, the quality of its service and its relaxed atmosphere, not to mention the presence of Nicola Marzouilla, the enthusiastic and knowledgeable owner. Chick pea fritters with wild mushrooms on a bed of prosciutto, baked oysters with pancetta and taleggio, baked macaroni stuffed with veal, chicken stuffed with a combination of prosciutto, veal and pecorino, braised rabbit, grilled swordfish with leeks and rosemary, flourless chocolate tart, espresso and bittersweet chocolate timbale, pinenut tart with vanilla gelato. Innovative wine list. $$$½ 🍷🍷🍷🍷

★★★ **LA COLOMBE D'OR**—134 East 26th Street (near Lexington Avenue)—689-0666—Now back in the hands of its creators, trailblazers Helen and George Studley (who briefly handed over the reins to restaurateurs Wayne Nish and Joseph Scalice), La Colombe D'Or returns to its roots as a traditional French bistro with Provençal flavorings. Its white-washed interior and eclectic paintings have been joined by a newly-decorated bar area upholstered in a hot tropical pattern, where cigar smoking is permitted. Potato and leek soup, cervelles with capers, goat cheese gnocchi with truffle oil, house-smoked skate with braised cabbage, grilled salmon with honey-mustard glaze, chef Naj Zougari's traditional cous cous, grilled spring lamb chops with zucchini, lemon sabayon tart, gateau victoire, walnut squares with Tahitian vanilla ice cream. $$$$½ 🍷🍷🍷

★★ **LES HALLES**—411 Park Avenue South (near 28th Street)—679-4111—This popular spot is an amiable and boisterous replication of a Parisian butcher shop/restaurant. It's true you can order free range chicken, but essentially, this is a carnivore's dream—hanger steak, entrecôte au poivre vert, cassoulet, boudin noir, French fries, and some exemplary fruit tarts. Service is hectic, and the place is always packed, so expect a wait for your table. The wine list has some interesting country bottlings. Take-out butcher service. $$$½ 🍷🍷

★★★ **NOVITA**—102 East 22nd Street (near Lexington Avenue)—677-2222—A minimalist, Milanese-style design prevails at this smart trattoria with yellow walls, flattering lighting and a willing service staff. Lombardian cooking is dominated by robust gastronomy, and Chef Marco Fregoneses' menu combines classic dishes as well as delectable specials. Risotto con gorgonzola, fazzoletti con vitello, duck prosciutto with foie gras and black truffles, sirloin with white beans and balsamic vinegar, involtini of chicken with porcini, panna cotta, tiramisù. $$$ 🍷🍷

★★½ **PARK AVALON**—225 Park Avenue South (corner 18th Street)—533-2500—A sprawling and animated place which by day attracts a downtown business crowd, but come nightfall transforms itself into a hip, candle-lit destination. No matter what the hour, you can count on satisfying fare and friendly service: Caesar salad, semolina crusted spicy calamari, chicken handroll with arugula, avocado and bacon, seared yellowfin tuna, BLT, pizzas, basil linguini, frozen yogurt in a mango sauce. $$ 🍷🍷🍷

★★★★ **PARK BISTRO**—414 Park Avenue South (near 28th Street)—689-1360—Anyone looking for a traditional French bistro need go no further. A zinc bar, leather banquettes, posters and photographs create just the right spirit. Chef/owner Jean-Michel Diot and partner Max Bernard run a bustling and crowded dining room, popular for its charm and for its authentic Provençal menu. Diot's pétatou de chevre frais—a stunning potato and goat cheese appetizer—remains a must-try. Take advantage of specials like stuffed calamari Basquaise, graavlax with potato blini, skate in Port wine, cod with meat jus and chips, chicken with garlic mashed potatoes, crème brûlée, apple tart. $$$$ 🍷🍷🍷

★★★★ **PATRIA**—250 Park Avenue South (corner 20th Street)—777-6211—From the warm welcome to the terrific paintings on the walls, a bustling bar scene and an exotic menu, Patria is a thoroughly electrifying experience. Chef Douglas Rodriguez's Latin American cuisine shines with more finesse than ever. He has focused his ingredients with superb results. Ecuadorian ceviche, crispy oysters with Huacatay sauce, black lobster empanada, sugarcane tuna with dried shrimp salsa, Patria pork with black bean broth and jalapeno vinegar, Chilean salmon with aji amarillo sauce, Colombian smoked ribeye. Crisp malarrabia—exotic tropical fruits with boniato and cookie crust—bananas tres leches, mango blackberry pudding with citrus cream. $$$$

★★½ **PITCHOUNE**—226 Third Avenue (corner 19th Street)—614-8641—You step through tropical-patterned curtains into a hip little spot with stenciled yellow walls, tin ceilings, bright plaid banquettes and vintage toys. The open kitchen delivers with considerable flair and prices are reasonable. The staff is cool, and the music is of the moment. The crowd has fun. Potato leek soup, toasted sweet breads, salmon tartare, monkfish with black pepper spaetzle, calf's liver with Savoy cabbage, warm apple clafouti, Armagnac prunes with vanilla ice cream. Dinner only and Sunday brunch. Visa and MasterCard only. $$½

★★★★½ **UNION SQUARE CAFE**—21 East 16th Street (between Fifth Avenue and Union Square West)—243-4020—Arguably the city's hottest destination, this kitchen reigns as one of Manhattan's finest. The eclectic decor, which was ahead of its time, remains timeless: cream-colored walls, vivid artwork, varied dining spaces and one of the best and longest bars in town. The dynamic and knowledgeable owner, Danny Meyer, has a knack for making every guest feel special, buttressed by the supremely talented Chef Michael Romano, who brings new meaning to Italian and American fare. The wait staff is impeccable, and genuine in their enthusiasm. Signature dishes like black bean soup, hot garlic potato chips are a must-try for the uninitiated. House smoked salmon with bean cakes, fried calamari with anchovy mayonnaise, porcini gnocchi with prosciutto and shiitakes, lamb rollatine with pine nuts and raisins, yellowfin tuna burger, bistecca alla Fiorentina, warm banana tart, chocolate devil's food cake, warm stuffed apple tart. Excellent wine cellar and wine-by-the-glass program. $$$$

★★★★ **VERBENA**—54 Irving Place (between 17th and 18th Streets)—260-5454—The somewhat condescending greeting at the door stands in marked contrast with the genial townhouse interior with pressed herbs and framed botanicals that lies within. Presided over by talented chef Diane Forley, whose American menus showcase seasonal ingredients, Verbena has become one of the city's most popular destinations, both for its stunning terrace garden in summer and cozy seats by the fireplace in winter. Butternut squash ravioli, sautéed foie gras, braised wild mushrooms with angel hair pasta, steamed halibut with fava beans, boneless squab with ragout of salsify, grilled filet mignon and chile-potato croquettes. Bittersweet chocolate soufflé, Verbena crème brûlée, panzotti with dried fruits. $$$$½ 🍷🍷🍷

★★★ **THE WATER CLUB**—500 East 30th Street (on the East River)—683-3333—While this gigantic, handsome barge hasn't the view of its sibling, The River Café, on the Brooklyn side, The Water Club has always been a delightful spot for a special evening. The greeting at the door is friendly and the captains are helpful, though service remains rudimentary. Chef Brad Steelman has introduced some imaginative dishes, but the large volume of customers and the banquet business somewhat compromises the kitchen. Seared sea scallops with portobello mushroom strudel, handmade cavatelli with tomato and basil, tasting of Moulard duck, seared tuna steak with scallion noodles, roasted rack of lamb with marjoram cous cous, pan roasted baby chicken with chestnut polenta, crème brûlée. $$$$ 🍷🍷🍷

★★½ **ZEN PALATE**—34 Union Square East (corner 16th Street)—614-9291—A branch transplant of the theater district original (with virtually the same menu), dramatic contemporary decor, and an unswerving dedication to Chinese vegetarian fare. In truth, if you are not fond of soy protein and soba noodles, this one's not for you; mini-mushroom "steak" will leave a true carnivore hankering for the real thing. Moo-Shu basil rolls, spinach rolls, sesame chips, sweet and sour pecans, dumplings. $$½ No liquor license.

FIFTEENTH TO THIRTY-FOURTH STREET (WEST)

★★★ **CAFFE BONDÍ**—7 West 20th Street (between Fifth Avenue and Avenue of the Americas)—691-8136—Having undergone a major renovation, the space is warmer and more refined-looking, and the furnishings are a lot more comfortable. But in the process, Bondi seems to have lost a bit of its pioneering spirit. The menu aspires to a level beyond trattoria basics, and the wine-by-the-glass program has been cut back. Nevertheless, Caffe Bondí remains a welcome addition to a neighborhood that is short on quality destinations. Eggplant rolls stuffed with pine nuts, taglierini with tomatoes, mushrooms and rosemary cream, ravioli filled with pumpkin and ricotta, schiacciata alle erbe, flourless chocolate cake, white chocolate crème brûlée, gelati. $$$ 🍷🍷

★★★ **CHELSEA BISTRO & BAR**—358 West 23rd Street (between 8th and 9th Avenues)—727-2026—A very cheerful spot with a stenciled ceiling, brick fireplace, brass rails, and prints dotting the walls. The staff is efficient and altogether unpretentious. The talented chef Philippe Roussel presides over the kitchen, preparing the likes of warm flan of wild mushrooms, carpaccio of salmon with ginger vinaigrette, cassoulette of snails, roasted cod with spinach, roasted marinated free range chicken, crème brûlée, chocolate extraveganza. $$$½ 🍷🍷🍷

★★★½ **DA UMBERTO**—107 West 17th Street (near Avenue of the Americas)—989-0303—With its rubbed yellow walls, vintage engravings, a boisterous bar room, and a glassed-in kitchen in back, Da Umberto has evolved into a finely tuned machine, overseen by the savvy Umberto Assante and family. This popular destination attracts a good-looking and lively crowd. Service is smart and affable. The kitchen is focused and well honed. Stuffed eggplant, glistening vegetable antipasto, risotto verde, salmon in mustard cream sauce, spiedino di scampi, spicy marinated baby chicken, tiramisù, chocolate mousse cake. $$$½ 🍷🍷🍷

★★½ **THE EMPIRE DINER**—210 Tenth Avenue (near 22nd Street)—243-2736—There's nothing like it in its category. A restored Deco showpiece, replete with Formica and chrome. Amusing cocktails, eclectic appetizers from hummus and barbecued chicken wings to nachos and wontons. Excellent chili sundae, BLT, blue plate specials. Pianist some nights. Good beer list. Casual. $$ 🍷

★★½ **FLOWERS**—21 West 17th Street (near Fifth Avenue)—691-8888—When Flowers opened it was a haunt for the pretty and the flighty, who always desert such places. After that crowd left, the kitchen, under Marc Salonsky, got serious and is now aiming for a more sophisticated clientele—who can nevertheless tolerate a decibel level that could turn Niagara Falls into white noise. Tuna tartare, bay scallop ravioli with minestrone sauce, mushroom soup with BBQ dumplings, BBQ sturgeon with orange vinaigrette, pecan-chocolate torte. $$$½ 🍷🍷

★★★★ **FOLLONICO**—6 West 24th Street (near Fifth Avenue)—691-6359—An unpretentious but extremely inviting trattoria, with rich wood paneling and beams, pale yellow walls, glowing sconces and a tiled wood-burning oven. Follonico sits on a landmark site, and chef Alan Tardi has created a marvelous new chapter. His food is original and exciting, yet easy-going. The wine list is interesting and well-priced. Deep fried oysters with horseradish cream and osetra caviar are a must. Wood-roasted calamari with garlic, carpaccio of tuna with sea urchin and radish sprouts, autumn leaf fazzoletto over wild mushroom ragoût with white truffle oil, casserole of rabbit and white beans, fricassee of lobster with mushrooms and polenta, filet of beef with trumpet mushrooms, granita of concord grape, fig in phyllo pastry, chocolate semifreddo. $$$½ 🍷🍷🍷

★★ **HOT TOMATO**—676 Sixth Avenue (corner 21st Street)—691-3535—Its red awning is a beacon for anyone craving huge portions of fun and satisfying fare. Tomato-like fixtures glow over a crowded bar (which serves eight beers on draft and another 75 by the bottle) and the walls are sponged in tobacco hues intermittently laced with ivy-patterned wallpaper. The music is loud and the staff scurries to keep it all moving. Go with a group or dine alone—this is an easy destination for everyone. Escarole and chicken noodle soup, vegetable pancakes with horseradish sour cream, roasted turkey sandwich with homemade gravy, flame-grilled burger, mix and match pastas, chicken pot pie, peanut butter pie, chocolate pudding. $$ 🍷🍷

★★★½ **LE MADRI**—168 West 18th Street (near Seventh Avenue)—727-8022—This trailblazing trattoria owned by the peripatetic Pino Luongo remains stylish and fresh-looking. With its cream-colored walls, green plaid chairs and innovative floral displays, the room has a dramatic effect. Chef Angelo Sessa is the latest talent to take over the range here (with Le Madri veteran Marta Pulini in the wings), and his Neapolitan fare is flavorful and generous. You can always count on a variety of pizzas from the wood burning oven. Timbale of pickled vegetables with buffalo mozzarella, casserole of calamari with tomatoes and scallions, ravioli with artichokes, pounded chicken breast with prosciutto, chopped sirloin of lamb with carrot and potato purée, chocolate panna cotta, cheesecake with orange sauce, praline pie. This is a great spot for a business lunch as service is not only knowledgeable, but prompt. $$$$ 🍷🍷🍷🍷

★★★★ **LOLA**—30 West 22nd Street (near Fifth Avenue)—675-6700—The shadowy room, the alluring crowd, and the live jazz and gospel music (a combination which may result in deafening decibel levels) make Lola one of the most vibrant restaurants in the city. Chef/owner Lynne Aronson is a master of spicing, and her highly innovative menu is a fusion of Caribbean, Mediterranean and Oriental dishes. Two-grain curry shrimp risotto, tomato-glazed tuna with black olive ratatouille, chile-rubbed grilled Black Angus with stuffed poblano pepper, Lola fried chicken with Cuban black beans, hoisin-glazed duck breast, grilled baby chicken with peanut broth, toasted caramel and coconut flan, Caribbean banana rum cheesecake, warm chocolate pecan tart. Sunday gospel brunch ($29.75) has a huge following. $$$$ 🍷🍷

★★★½ **LUMA**—200 Ninth Avenue (at 22nd Street)—633-8033—This small and soothing pastel-hued space with soft lighting has a Chelsea amiability about it. It is presided over by chef-partner Scott Bryan, who comes to Luma after stints at Bouley, Lespinasse, Le Bernardin and Gotham Bar & Grill. He favors reductions and grilling to sautéeing and frying, and his food has a lovely translucent quality and a keen sense of refinement. "Oversized" mushroom ravioli with mascarpone and herb broth, Asian tuna tartare with crisp potatoes, roasted sweetbreads with shiitakes, five-spice halibut with pea shoots, vegetable risotto with white truffle oil, Valrhona chocolate soufflé, lemon millefeuille. $$$½ 🍷🍷🍷

★★★½ **MESA GRILL**—102 Fifth Avenue (near 15th Street)—807-7400—Owner Jerry Kretchmer (he also co-owns Gotham Bar and Grill and Judson Bar and Grill, q.v.) has turned these former bank premises into a boisterous, colorful eatery, full of tall columns, artsy photographs, and a good bar area, all quite apt for chef Bobby Flay's exciting Southwest-inspired food. Every dish has lots of flavor, lots of color, and zip. This is a complete package—an amusing atmosphere, a smart-looking crowd, and novel cuisine. Very noisy however, especially upstairs. White bean and roasted tomato soup, tuna tartare with plantains, barbecued lamb rib and white bean salad, grilled mahi mahi in green chile coconut broth, blue corn salmon cakes, gingerbread ice cream sandwich, vanilla buñuelo. $$$½ 🍷🍷

★★★ **THE OLD HOMESTEAD**—56 Ninth Avenue (at 15th Street)—242-9040—Claiming to be the oldest steakhouse in NYC, The Old Homestead still has some antique charm in the barroom area, though the non-smoking tables are in a dreadfully kitschy room with palette-knife paintings and ersatz brick walls. The steaks and prime rib are of unstintingly fine quality, and the astoundingly rich Japanese Kobe beef is unique on these shores. The vegetable beef soup is excellent, the prime rib is massive. While the 10-ounce serving of Kobe beef goes for $100, why not order the Kobe sampler at just $21, then move on to U.S. prime steak? $$$$ 🍷

★★★ **PERIYALI**—35 West 20th Street (near Avenue of the Americas)—463-7890—The greeting here is as warm as ever, and the place still fills with an enthusiastic crowd hungry for out-of-the-ordinary Greek fare. While Periyali remains true to its traditions, the kitchen is not always innovative, and some dishes seem a bit routine. Calamari with caviar mousse dip, grilled eggplant salad, puréed yellow split pea salad, chicken and fennel brochette, baked shrimp with tomatoes, scallions and feta, moussaka, charcoal-grilled lamb shish kebob. $$$ 🍷🍷

★★½ **TRAMPS CAFÉ**—45 West 21st Street (between 5th Avenue and Avenue of the Americas)—633-9570—Abe de la Houssaye (ex Texarcana and La Louisiana), presides over this long dark space with sponged walls, and an open kitchen. Expect honest, Cajun fare, served up in a casual, friendly manner. Crawfish are a specialty here, flown in daily from Louisiana in season. Crab and sausage gumbo, fried oysters, shrimp étouffée, Po' boy sandwiches, fried okra, red beans and rice, chocolate Jeremy. $$½ 🍷

★★★ **ZUCCA**—227 Tenth Avenue (corner 23rd Street)—741-1970—This Chelsea destination sports a chic, convivial bar and a good-looking dining room. Service is friendly, and the atmosphere is relaxed. Zucca means pumpkin in Italian, so it's no surprise that pumpkins pop up throughout chef Eric Stapelman's Mediterranean menu. Pumpkin soup, Hudson Valley foie gras with grilled figs, grilled portobello mushroom with soft polenta, duck confit with roasted plum tomatoes, pan-roasted free-range chicken with chestnut mashed potatoes, boneless New York strip steak with pumpkin purée, rack of Australian lamb with ragoût of vegetables, pumpkin crème brûlée, gelati. $$$½ 🍷🍷🍷

THIRTY-FIFTH TO FIFTIETH STREET (EAST)

★★★ **AL BUSTAN**—827 Third Avenue (near 50th Street)—759-5933—A simple interior with white walls and tablecloths, landscape watercolors, and tall vases bursting with flowers. Al Bustan, which means "the orchard," offers a broad spectrum of Lebanese dishes, rich in flavor and texture. The staff is most helpful in assisting with menu suggestions and are both friendly and attentive. Why not make a meal out of the delectable hot and cold appetizers? Hummus, baba ghannouj, warak inab (grape leaves stuffed with rice and tomatoes), mouhamara (puréed walnuts with red peppers, garlic and chilis), makanek (sauted lamb sausages), safiha (baked pastry with minced meat, tomatoes and pignoli nuts), falafel. Main courses such as lamb medallions or baked Cornish hen can be heavy. Tasty pastries. Take-out too. $$$ 🍷🍷

★★½ **AMBASSADOR GRILL**—1 U.N. Plaza (near First Avenue at 44th Street in the U.N. Plaza Hotel)—702-5014—With its mirrored ceiling, frame-backed chairs and checkerboard floor, Ambassador Grill is a quiet oasis hiding in the shadow of the United Nations. We

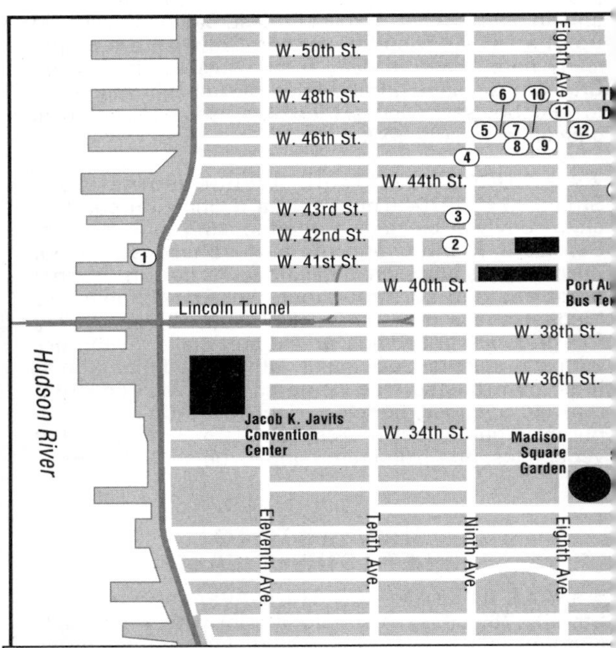

THIRTY-FIFTH TO FIFTIETH STREET (WEST)

1 World Yacht Cruises
2 Chez Josephine
3 Frico Bar
4 Jezebel
5 Zen Palate
6 Becco
7 Barbetta
8 Joe Allen
9 Orso
10 Firebird
11 B. Smith's
12 Coco Pazzo Teatro
13 Sardi's
14 Un Deux Trois
15 Virgil's Barbecue
16 Osteria Al Doge
17 Keen's
18 Bryant Park
19 Café 44
20 Torre di Pisa
21 The Rainbow Room
22 Sea Grill
23 La Réserve
24 American Festival Café

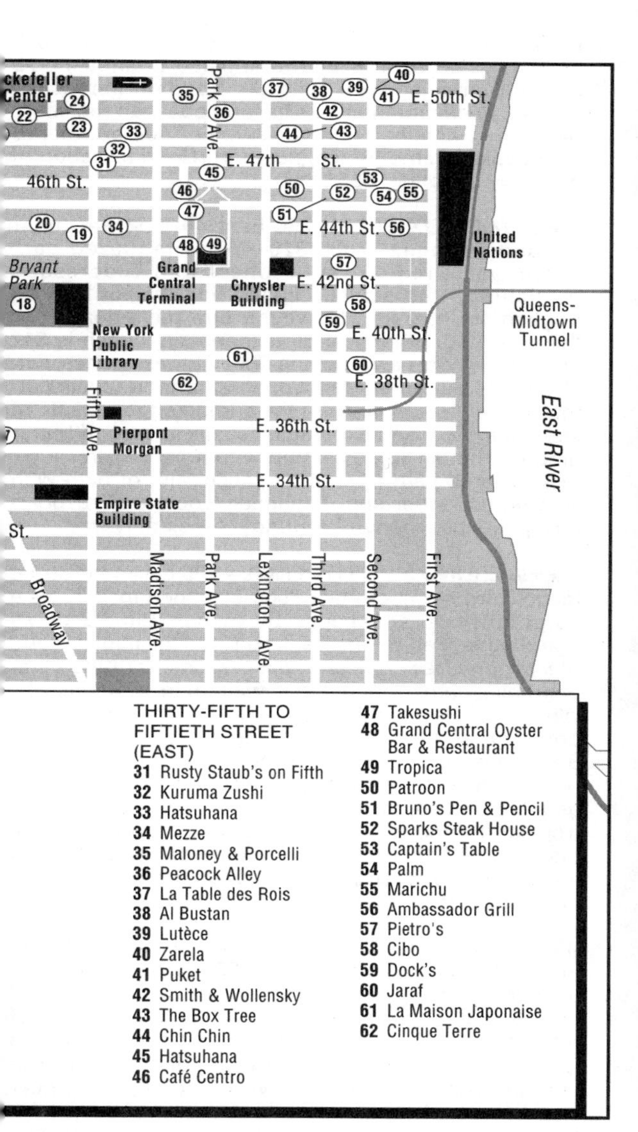

THIRTY-FIFTH TO FIFTIETH STREET (EAST)

31 Rusty Staub's on Fifth
32 Kuruma Zushi
33 Hatsuhana
34 Mezze
35 Maloney & Porcelli
36 Peacock Alley
37 La Table des Rois
38 Al Bustan
39 Lutèce
40 Zarela
41 Puket
42 Smith & Wollensky
43 The Box Tree
44 Chin Chin
45 Hatsuhana
46 Café Centro
47 Takesushi
48 Grand Central Oyster Bar & Restaurant
49 Tropica
50 Patroon
51 Bruno's Pen & Pencil
52 Sparks Steak House
53 Captain's Table
54 Palm
55 Marichu
56 Ambassador Grill
57 Pietro's
58 Cibo
59 Dock's
60 Jaraf
61 La Maison Japonaise
62 Cinque Terre

prefer to make a meal of the creative first courses, such as warm sea scallops with marinated potatoes, crab and lobster salad with avocado, bourbon barbecued shrimp. Pricey main dishes include poached red snapper, loin of antelope and venison. For dessert, there's opera cake, crème brûlée, pear tart. Good selection of wines by the glass. $$$$ 🍷🍷

★★½ **THE BOX TREE**—250 East 49th Street (near Second Avenue)—758-8320—With its glazed dark green walls, red shaded sconces and Tudoresque furnishing, this eclectic space has the look of an English country inn. However, one pays dearly for this charmed, other worldly experience. Lunch is $42 and dinner costs a whopping $86! At these prices, service could be more attentive, and the food, while correctly executed, is far from the cutting edge. Terrine of leeks, eggplant and asparagus, snails in Pernod butter gratinée, house cured salmon with horseradish sauce, rack of lamb with fresh mint sauce, filet of beef with cracked coriander and Armagnac, cocotte of raspberries, pears poached in Burgundy. Amex only. 🍷🍷🍷

★★★½ **BRUNO'S PEN & PENCIL**—205 East 45th Street (near Third Avenue)—682-8660—Opened in 1932 as a neighborhood speakeasy by owner John Bruno's grandfather, Pen & Pencil still conveys the genial mood of a bygone New York era—dark woods, sporting paraphernalia, comfy banquettes, waiters in white jackets. While customers still flock here for first-rate steaks, prime rib and lamb chops, in deference to the times, Bruno has introduced a spa menu listing the fat, calorie and cholesterol count of select items ranging from genuine buffalo-burger (5 g. fat, 234 cal., 106 chol.) to tropical fruit soup (1 g. fat, 159 cal., 0 chol.). For the unconcerned, there's also excellent Caesar salad, lentil and vegetable soup, crab cakes. $29.75 pre-theater dinner. $$$$½ 🍷🍷🍷

★★★ **CAFÉ CENTRO**—200 Park Avenue (at 45th Street in the Met Life Building)—818-1222—A vast space with the bustling energy of a cafeteria, Café Centro is divided into several rooms, all eclectically done up with a bit of retro this and deco that. It is an ideal spot for a business lunch or a pre-theater dinner because of its central location, prompt and friendly service. The adjoining beer bar, with a vast selection, is also a great bet for a quick bite. Portions are generous, and the French/Moroccan fare is varied and satisfying. New chef Stephane Becht has preserved the traditions of his predecessor, with such appealing additions as chicken salad Chinoise and lobster avocado club. Chicken and mushroom brique, goat cheese and vegetable tart, steak frites, vegetable cous cous, almond macaroons, warm apple tartlette. Reservations a must. $$$½ 🍷🍷🍷

★★★ **CAPTAIN'S TABLE**—860 Second Avenue (at 46th Street)—697-9538—This midtown place (more popular at lunchtime) is staffed by a particularly genial bunch, from the amiable owner, Gino Musso, to the busboys. It's an excellent spot to sample the freshest fish and seafood, prepared in either a traditional or contemporary manner. Breaded shrimp with jalapeño and mozzarella, broiled halibut with aïoli or diavolo sauce, scallops, red snapper. The Captain's Table also features a take-out counter, where you can purchase fish for preparation at home. $$$½ 🍷🍷

★★★ **CHIN CHIN**—216 East 49th Street (near Third Avenue)—888-4555—Vintage photographs snapped in the Far East at the turn of the century, juxtaposed with bleached walls, plush banquettes, and dramatic lighting create a sleek, stark look. But the atmosphere at Chin Chin after work can be boisterous. Nevertheless, the kitchen's output compensates for the din. Pan fried dumplings, scallion pancake, lobster roll, mai fun, tea-smoked Cornish game hen, shredded pork, chicken Tung, orange beef. $$$½ 🍷🍷🍷

★★½ **CIBO**—767 Second Avenue (corner 41st Street)—681-1616—Located in one of those busy neighborhoods where lunch is always better attended than dinner, Cibo is a popular new restaurant with an upbeat and relaxed atmosphere, widely separated tables and a promising young chef, K. Tyler Florence. His New York–Italian fare makes up in quantity what it lacks in finesse. Steamed Manila clams with a combination of leeks, tomato and pancetta, pan-seared striped bass with whipped potatoes, roast duck with Savoy cabbage and huckleberries, ginger crème brûlée, apple-almond tart. $$$½ 🍷🍷🍷

★★★½ **CINQUE TERRE**—22 East 38th Street (between Madison and Park Avenues)—213-0910—To experience the verdant cooking of Liguria, book a table at the intimate Cinque Terre (aptly named after the five fishing villages perched atop the Italian Riviera). The place is vibrant and vivacious with buttery yellow walls and deep blue accents. Owners Mario Massa and Francesco Rabellino pride themselves on recreating the authentic food of the region. Their pesto sauce with potatoes and string beans is perfection. Pansotti with herbs and walnut sauce, pappardelle with rabbit and mushrooms, squid stew Ligurian style, cotechino with lentils, lemon-herbed chicken, warm apple tart. $$$½ 🍷🍷

★★½ **DOCK'S**—633 Third Avenue (near 40th Street)—986-8080—An East Side branch of a West Side original, this is an honest seafood house with a pleasant atmosphere, white-tiled walls, and a large central bar. The menu is somewhat predictable, but you can expect good clam chowder, stone crab claws, and a nice selection of daily specials such as broiled grouper or grilled mahi mahi, plus hefty desserts like chocolate mud cake and apple pie. $$$$ 🍷🍷

Ö ★★★½ **GRAND CENTRAL OYSTER BAR & RESTAURANT**—Grand Central Terminal—490-6650—Opened in 1912, this veteran American seafood restaurant is renowned for its extraordinary offerings of oysters and virtually every kind of fish that has ever been offered at the Fulton Market. An astounding space to eat in (underneath the Terminal's Great Hall), it is always crowded at lunch (less so at dinner) but you can escape the din at the "saloon" in the rear. Choose from a dozen varieties of fresh oysters, or opt for the fried variety. Sample the smoked sturgeon, fried squid, Florida stone crabs, Maine lobster club sandwich, seared filet of North Atlantic tuna with cayenne mayonnaise. Leave room for the nesselrode pie. Over 60 wines, primarily American Chardonnay, are available by the glass. Closed Saturday and Sunday. $$$$ 🍷🍷🍷🍷

★★½ **HATSUHANA**—237 Park Avenue (on 46th St)—661-3400—and 17 East 48th Street (near Madison Avenue)—355-3345—The original location on 48th Street is pleasant enough, while the Park Avenue branch (actually wedged off the Avenue between the streets) is prettier, with a greenhouse dining room. At both places you'll find Japanese businessmen at the sushi bar or tables challenging the itamae chef to come up with something interesting. He always does—from mackerel and pickled ginger to broiled squid feet. For those with more conservative tastes, there is good tempura, sashimi, and salmon teriyaki. Service can be haphazard. $$$$½ 🍷

★★½ **JARAF**—720 Second Avenue (between 38th and 39th Streets)—696-1654—We keep hearing that Murray Hill is the next hot new destination, and maybe that's why chef James Rafferty located his cozy, brick-walled restaurant with the portmanteau name there. Trained at Taillevent in Paris, Le Gavroche in London, and Bouley in New York, he shows excellent control and good taste in dishes like potato and blue cheese cake, roasted lamb with homemade spaetzle and Port wine sauce, pan-seared bass with perfectly tender vegetables, and chocolate crème brûlée. $$$ 🍷

★★★★ **KURUMA ZUSHI**—7 East 47th Street (between Madison and 5th Avenues)—317-2802—Tucked away on the second floor of a midtown office building (there's an elevator if you don't want to walk up) is this sparse space with burgundy tables and black fan-backed chairs, presided over by Toshihiro Uezu. You may opt for the popular sushi bar, or two very good-looking tatami (private dining) rooms. The sparkling quality and flawless presentation of the sushi and sashimi along with helpful and unpretentious service make this a self-indulging experience. Fresh sea urchins, monkfish paté, grated radish with mushrooms, pickled vegetables, chopped yellowtail with scallions, toro tuna, abalone, scallops, Japanese prawns, California roll, green tea ice cream. Fixed price sushi and sashimi assortments start at $19. $$$ 🍷

★★½ **LA MAISON JAPONAISE**—125 East 39th Street (between Park and Lexington Avenues)—682-7375—This subtle room with cane-backed chairs, burgundy upholstery and crisp white tablecloths derives its personality from a whimsical window display at street level and a dramatic floral arrangement in back. Expect low-key, easy dining. The kitchen serves up generous portions of Japanese/French fare, and the staff is well-intended but slow. Shumai dumplings, miso soup, hot seafood salad, filet of tuna on portabello mushrooms with soba noodles, loin of lamb on toasted bread crumbs, poached pear, Mount Fuji sundae. The $17.95 fixed price lunch is an absolute steal. $$$ 🍷🍷

★★½ **LA TABLE DES ROIS**—135 East 50th Street (near Third Avenue)—838-7275—A pleasant, unpretentious and satisfying alternative to many midtown eateries, nicely suited to a business lunch or a pre-theater dinner (the latter is available at a fixed price of $20.50). You can count on well executed bistro fare—salade aux lardons, soup à l'oignon, pâtés and terrines, plus crab cakes with Pernod butter, grilled salmon with lemon grass, veal sautéed with Calvados and apples, crème caramel. $$$ 🍷🍷 Fixed price $20.50 dinner.

★★★★½ **LUTÈCE**—249 East 50th Street (near Second Avenue)—752-2225—In 1995, the legendary André Soltner sold his bastion of French cuisine to Michael Weinstein of the Ark Corporation, who hired Eberhardt Mueller to carry on the traditions. The restaurant has been completely renovated and sports a color scheme of muted yellows, mottled peaches and burnt siennas. The garden room is enchanting, with light colored lattice-work finials and greenery, and the upstairs has been revamped, complete with a romantic balcony. Formerly executive chef at Le Bernardin, Mueller is at his best with seafood but is no slouch with meat and poultry. The charming veteran staff remains thankfully intact, presided over by Janet Cam, and the wine list has been greatly improved. Fresh cèpes salad, potato and leek soup, "club sandwich" of fresh foie gras with apple compote, monkfish braised with bacon topped by pearl onions and tomatoes, grilled squab over lentils with white truffles, breast of duck with herbed polenta and a compote of sweet Vidalia onions, pineapple fruit soup, plum tart with vanilla ice cream, roasted apricots in phyllo with an apricot sorbet. Fixed price lunch $38. Fixed price dinner $65. 🍷🍷🍷🍷🍷

★★★½ **MALONEY & PORCELLI**—37 East 50th Street (between Park and Madison Avenues)—750-2233—The vast space which was once Gloucester has been entirely renovated in the New York Restaurant Group's signature style—warm woods and an attractive sprinkling of Americana. This instant institution feels as if it has been here forever. The menu was devised by Park Avenue Café's David Burke and is capably executed by chef Patrick Vacarriello. While you can feast on a bevy of oversize steaks, chops and lobsters, you can also opt for more innovative fare such as thin-crust pizza, crabcakes with ratatouille, Caesar salad with lemon confit, mushroom hash, mustard-crusted tuna steak, and a hands-down winner, crackling pork shank. Delectable desserts include drunken donuts, wood-oven apple tart with vanilla ice cream. A well constructed wine list includes a special listing of forty wines under $40.

★★½ **MARICHU**—342 East 46th Street (between First and Second Avenues)—370-1866—This cozy interior with exposed brick walls dotted with decorative plates specializes in Basque cuisine. The menu reads well, but is presented with a surprising lack of enthusiasm. Andalusian gazpacho, shrimp in garlic sauce, cannelloni of spinach and shrimp with tomato sauce, chicken breast with scalloped potatoes, red Rioja peppers stuffed with purée of bacalao in salsa Vizcaina. Decent flan, leche frito. $$$ 🍷🍷🍷

★★★ **MEZZE**—10 East 44th Street (between Madison and Fifth Avenues)—697-6644—From the moment the peripatetic Matthew Kenney (Matthew's, q.v. and Monzu) opened his Mediterranean/Moroccan take-out and canteen, customers have been lining up to sample the appealing and inexpensive fare. Mezze's superb flatbread plays an important role on the menu, which includes flatbread pizza topped by grilled artichokes with onion confit and rosemary, flatbread sandwiches such as charcoal-grilled vegetables with humus, and flatbread salad with tomato, cucumber and feta. Consider Moroccan-spiced carrots with cumin, Mediterranean chicken salad, warm shrimp and white bean salad with confit of artichokes, cardamon- and yogurt-marinated lamb. Mezze offers a variety of pastries for dessert. No liquor license. $½

⏱ ★★★½ **PALM**—837 Second Avenue (at 45th Street)—687-2953—Since 1926, Palm has defined the New York steakhouse genre with its no-nonsense approach to American dining. The amusing caricatures of regular patrons, the hustle and bustle of waiters balancing enormous platters, and the feeling that you have come of age by dining here make this a wonderful slice of New York life. Prices are a bit lower than at some other steakhouses around town. Across the street, Palm Too (with ten branches around the U.S.) is just as good if less historic. Tomatoes and onions, 17-ounce aged sirloins, broiled lobsters, cottage fries, S&S cheesecake. $$$$½ 🍷🍷

★★★½ **PATROON**—160 East 46th Street (between Lexington and Third Avenues)—883-7373—The site that once housed Christ Cella, the landmark steakhouse, has been reborn as Patroon (Dutch for landowner) with Ken Aretsky (he also owns Butterfield '81) as proprietor. He presides over a monochromatic space with gray faux-Fortuny fabrics, taupe banquettes and subdued lighting which vaguely resembles a private Pullman car. The staff is efficient and a tad too eager to please. Patroon's appeal also derives from several cigar-friendly salons upstairs with massive humidor facilities and a handsome downstairs bar. The menu, executed by chef Franck Deletrain (ex-Four Seasons) proffers numerous alternatives to an expensive steak (wood grilled porterhouse for two is $75) and a shrimp cocktail: smoked sea scallops with beets, wild mushroom risotto, gravlaax with maple mustard vinaigrette, lamb chops with eggplant polenta, peppered tuna with soba noodle salad, salmon with wild mushroom hash, chocolate malted Napoleon, apple tart, toasted coconut cake. Diners on a budget should seriously consider the $39.50 fixed price dinner. $$$$$ 🍷🍷🍷🍷

★★★★ **PEACOCK ALLEY**—301 Park Avenue (at 50th Street in The Waldorf-Astoria Hotel)—872-4895—In its original manifestation in the old Waldorf on 34th Street and Fifth Avenue, Peacock Alley catered to the first families of New York and was the place to see and be seen. Under the guidance of talented Gascon chef Laurent Manrique, whose special touch with foie gras and truffles is exemplary, this is now a place to dine exceedingly well. The paneled room with its lamplit tables has recently been revamped, but it still exudes a hotel-like atmosphere. The star here is Manrique's innovative cuisine. The staff is proud of the seasonal menu and most willing to please. Tartare of Pemaquid oysters with osetra caviar, chestnut soup with duck sausage and foie gras and truffled poultry quenelle, Maine diver sea scallops with black truffles and celeri remoulade, ravioli of foie gras, foie gras tasting plates, guinea hen with black truffle, caramelized endive and salsify, braised Scottish hare with foie gras and black truffles, poached free-range chicken with Gascon stuffing, quince desserts, pineapple macadamia, warm chocolate cake, apple dessert, fig dessert. Creative wine list. $$$$$ 🍷🍷🍷🍷

★★★ **PIETRO'S**—232 East 43rd Street (between Second and Third Avenues)—682-9760—A true New York institution, this former speakeasy (originally located on 45th Street) has been going strong since 1932. It is still home to some of the finest steaks in town, along with an exceptionally good Caesar salad. Alternatively, the chopped steak, and Southern Italian specialties like spaghetti with meat balls, are hearty, but a bit dated. Good cheesecake. $$$ 🍷

★★ **PUKET**—945 Second Avenue (near 50th Street)—759-6339—A touch of Thailand tucked in midtown Manhattan, Puket has evolved a pleasing and authentic formula, but one which has become a tad routine over time. Friendly service and an inviting interior set the stage nonetheless. Fried wonton, prawns, all satés, sautéed beef with red pepper and onions, deep fried fish, fried rice noodle with chicken and crushed peanuts. Festive cocktails. $$$ 🍷

★★★ **RUSTY STAUB'S ON FIFTH**—575 Fifth Avenue (enter on 47th Street)—682-1000—This clubby and cordial establishment, owned by former baseball player-turned-restaurateur Rusty Staub, boasts a serious and eclectic menu that far transcends the stereotypical athlete's regime of meat and potatoes. New Orleans-style gumbo, pizza with caramelized onions, baked goat cheese and lamb's lettuce, pecan crusted halibut, baby-back ribs, shrimp le grand orange, deep-dish apple pie. The wine list (Staub is a major player on the fine wine auction circuit) is spectacular. In addition to rare bottlings, you'll also find a copious selection of wines by the glass. $$$ 🍷🍷🍷🍷

★★★★ **SMITH & WOLLENSKY**—797 Third Avenue (at 49th Street)—753-1530—A very large, handsome, oak-floored steak-and-seafood house that is clearly a mid-town institution. The steaks, veal chops, lobsters, and seafood are all top quality, and the wine list is quite extraordinary, especially in vintage claret and Cabernet Sauvignon. (Owner Alan Stillman boasts a $1 million wine cellar containing over 42,000 bottles.) Service is brisk but adequate to the job, and this place is jammed day and night, as is the more casual grill to the rear. Thanks to late night hours, it also attracts an after-theater crowd. Great for private parties. Outdoor dining in the summer. A very New York "joint." $$$$½ 🍷🍷🍷🍷🍷

★★★★ **SPARKS STEAK HOUSE**—210 East 46th Street (near Third Avenue)—687-4855—With its upscale, saloon-like atmosphere, Sparks remains a midtown fixture for hearty fare. Pat Cetta's brilliant and well-priced wine list is the perfect complement to generous portions of beef rolled out of the kitchen on white-clothed carts. Service is almost mechanical, however. Oysters, lump crabmeat and bay scallops, baked clams, and tomato and onion salad pretty much sum up the appetizers. Grilled sirloin, filet mignon, extra-thick loin of veal chops and our favorite, steak fromage, will appeal to any carnivore. There's also a sprinkling of fish and seafood, ranging from enormous lobsters to swordfish and scallops. Vegetables are extra. Cheesecake remains the ideal finale. $$$$$ 🍷🍷🍷🍷🍷

★★★ **TAKESUSHI**—71 Vanderbilt Avenue (near 45th Street)—867-5120—This pretty, rambling room, with its blond wood, bright lights (to highlight the pristine freshness of the food) and widely separated tables make this an ideal choice in the midtown area for lunch, pre-theater supper or a leisurely dinner, either at the sushi counter or at the regular tables. For two decades now, TakeSushi has been more than dependable, more than consistent and more than reasonable. Complete dinners at $25–$35 are a good way to sample the kitchen's range. Grilled squid, deep-fried yam, softshell crab, ankimo monkfish liver, fried eggplant with miso paste, sashimi, sushi, tempura. $$$ 🍷

★★★ **TROPICA**—200 Park Avenue (enter on 45th Street in the Met Life Building Concourse)—867-6767—Many have regarded this convenient place situated above Grand Central Station as no more than a lunch stop and a place to have a nibble and a drink before heading home. Tropica has developed a following for a delectable seafood cuisine. Crab cakes with field greens and mustard beurre blanc, conch chowder with christophene and okra, grilled Arctic char with vegetable risotto, barbecued shrimp with Szechuan peppercorns and Hawaiian rice, kumquat mousse. Fixed price dinner is $29.00. $$$$ 🍷🍷🍷

★★★ **ZARELA**—953 Second Avenue (near 50th Street)—644-6740—This space is creative owner Zarela Martinez' personal celebration with its festive colors and convivial atmosphere. Though service can be a bit lackluster, the authentic Mexican cuisine (no clichés here) more than compensates. Fried calamari with pickled jalapeño sauce, chilaquiles verdes, pollo borracho, poblano relleno, fajitas, shrimp in jalapeño, onion and cilantro sauce, salmon ahumado, pecado michu (whole grilled trout with chipotle paste), Quetzalcoatlis chocolate "sin." $$$ 🍷🍷

THIRTY-FIFTH TO FIFTIETH STREET (WEST)

★★½ **AMERICAN FESTIVAL CAFÉ**—20 West 50th Street (in Rockefeller Center)—332-7620—This is a great place for a family outing. Set right on Rockefeller Center skating rink under the gaze of Prometheus and the umbrella of skyscrapers, the dining room is decorated with fine folk art in a casual, amiable way. The food reflects American classics. A great place at Christmastime under that famous tree. Service more efficient than it used to be, too. Steaks, Prime rib, crabcakes with cole slaw, key lime pie, strawberry shortcake. $$$ 🍷🍷

★★ **B. SMITH'S**—771 Eighth Avenue (at 47th Street)—247-2222—Owned by the dynamic former model Barbara Smith, this continues to be a popular theater district hangout. The interior, with its copper-colored columns, flame-stitched banquettes and a multi-hued mural is strangely simple; the crowd that fills the place gives it personality. The menu has portions for every appetite and budget. Roasted tomato soup with pesto, calamari with onion marmalade, duck sausage lasagna, spiced scampi with fried plantains, profiteroles, sweet potato pecan pie. Service can be haphazard. $$$ 🍷🍷

🍎★★★★ **BARBETTA**—321 West 46th Street (near Eighth Avenue)—246-9171—Now celebrating its 91st season, this is NYC's oldest family-run Italian restaurant. Every great musician and actor has dined here, including Toscanini. Presided over by the indefatigable Laura Maioglio, the exquisite townhouse setting encompasses a double-width dining room and garden. The former is decorated in superb period style. The latter is an enchanting oasis for warm weather dining—unquestionably the most extraordinary in the city. Upstairs are smart private dining salons. The kitchen is now more refined than ever. Salad of roasted beets with lola rosa, butterfly pasta with peas, cannelloni alla Savoirda, charcoal grilled swordfish over a bed of lentils, roasted rabbit in white wine sauce, beef braised in red wine with fagioli, roasted loin of veal in a tuna mayonnaise, panna cotta, fruit soup, dessert wagon. Pre-theater dinner is $39. $$$$$ 🍷🍷🍷🍷

★★★½ **BECCO**—355 West 46th Street (near Ninth Avenue)—397-7597—Clearly the most creative trattoria in the Theater District, Becco is a joy for all budgets. Joseph Bastianich (his parents run the deluxe Felidia, q.v.) offers set menus of antipasti and pasta for a fixed price of $16.95 at lunch and $19.95 at dinner, optionally followed by a variety of main courses and desserts for only a few dollars more. A glistening array of freshly grilled vegetables and superb pastas such as mushroom risotto, basil gnocchi, and pappardelle with rabbit stew may be followed by main courses such as osso buco, swordfish with balsamic vinegar, and spit-roasted suckling pig. Desserts, such as bread pudding with green apple sorbet, are moderately priced and include coffee. What's more, there are 15 wines offered at only $18 a bottle. $$$ 🍷🍷

★★ **BRYANT PARK GRILL**—25 West 40th Street (between Fifth Avenue and Avenue of the Americas)—840-6500—It took the Ark Restaurant Corporation to transform this hitherto dark and desolate space into one of the most captivating parks in New York with a handsome, contemporary-looking installation abutting the majestic New York Public Library. There's an outdoor café in season, and the indoor Grill is a lively spot for lunch. Too bad the rather pricey and highly eclectic menu doesn't live up to the decor and landscape, though the roasted chicken is as good as ever. $$$$ 🍷🍷🍷

★★★½ **CAFÉ 44**—44 West 44th Street (near Fifth Avenue in the Royalton Hotel)—869-4400—A polished marble entranceway and massive doors serve as an apt introduction to Philippe Starck's unique and austere decor. Although no longer sparkling, the place still generates electricity. Waiters dressed in black (what else?) merge with identically garbed customers. Café 44 remains a destination for power lunches and pre-theater dinners, with a lively bar scene in the evenings. Talented chef Jeffrey Zakarian is now back behind the range and the food has improved. Caesar salad, charred lamb sausage, goat cheese profiteroles, tuna foie gras, cod pot roast, venison loin, crisp polenta hash browns, calamari fritti, desserts. $$$$ 🍷🍷

★★½ **CHEZ JOSEPHINE**—414 West 42nd Street (near Ninth Avenue)—594-1925—Jean-Claude Baker has created the ultimate valentine to his adopted mother, the celebrated chanteuse Josephine Baker. The space is flamboyantly festooned in red velvet with bright blue tin ceilings, shirred window treatments and dazzling portraits of the restaurant's namesake. Mr. Baker is one of the city's most enthusiastic hosts. His staff is exceedingly loyal and service is very congenial. Napoleon of warm asparagus with shiitake mushrooms, Chinese ravioli with goat cheese, crispy oysters on a bed of fennel, excellent boudin noir with red cabbage and apple-onion compote, Elvira's down-home fried chicken with sweet potato fries, scallop and shrimp risotto with collard greens, black-and-white chocolate mousse, warm apple and rhubarb crêpe cake, bombe praline. $$$½ 🍷🍷

★★★ **COCO PAZZO TEATRO**—243 West 46th Street (near Eight Avenue in the Paramount Hotel)—827-4222—The latest addition to Pino Luongo's restaurant realm (Le Madri, Coco Pazzo, Il Toscanaccio, q.v.), this outpost in the theater district is less expensive and more casual than its 74th Street counterpart. Blue walls, light woods and a particularly genial staff put you instantly at ease. Swordfish carpaccio, pizza bianca with robiola cheese, overstuffed meat ravioli, roasted cornish hen with artichokes, navarin of lamb, Coca Pazzo fries, chocolate-covered ginger tartuffo, watermelon parfait. $$$ 🍷🍷🍷

★★★½ **FIREBIRD**—365 West 46th Street (between Eighth and Ninth Avenues)—586-0244—This is truly a Russian fantasy. The facade is indescribably grand, the interior worthy of a Grand Duke. With deep plush walls, opulent tapestries and glorious gilded details, the design is an obvious labor of love. We prefer the "library room," filled with rare books, vintage czarist photos and as a final touch, a golden apple tree. The staff, decked out in Cossack smocks, is charming and meticulous. Chef Brian Goode's classic Russian menu is immensely satisfying. Zakuska (small dishes) such as eggplant caviar, mushrooms with sour cream, roasted beets and Armenian braised artichokes. Alternate starters include lamb dumplings and herring under a blanket. Grilled sturgeon, karsky shaslik (grilled lamb) Uzbek skewered quail, double chocolate cake, poached comice pear, fruit-and-cheese-filled blini. $$$ 🍷🍷

★★★ **FRICO BAR**—402 West 43rd Street (corner Ninth Avenue)—564-7272—Once again, the Bastianich family (Felidia, Becco) have created another crowd pleaser. This contemporary space is the most casual of their restaurant trio. It is fun, lively, and best of all, offers tremendous value along with real originality. The menu and wine list are colorful and highly satisfying. Be sure to try one of the signature Fricos—a torte made of montasio (cow's milk cheese) with fillings such as potato, onions, sausage or greens. Consider the raw bar, fried calamari with spicy marinara sauce, baked ziti, luganiga sausage with mixed greens and Borlotti beans, braised venison with barley risotto, chocolate mousse cake, bread pudding, gelati. $$½ 🍷🍷🍷

★★½ **JEZEBEL**—630 Ninth Avenue (enter on 45th Street)—582-1045—This is theater in the theater district. The interior is seduction Southern-style, with crystal chandeliers, profuse candlelight, plenty of lace, suspended fringed shawls, Oriental carpets, and of course, live piano music. Dine on generous portions of tangy rib bits, spicy pea soup, Charleston she-crab soup, honey chicken, Carolina shrimp creole, smothered pork chops, banana pudding with Grand Marnier, chocolate fudge cake. The mood is relaxed, so take your time and savor the evocative setting. $$$ 🍷

★★ **JOE ALLEN**—326 West 46th Street (near Eighth Avenue)—581-6464—A long-time hangout for theatergoers and actors, Joe Allen has no pretensions and pretty decent, simple food. The ribs and burgers are dependable, the service affable (often by actors between jobs), and the place buzzes with a certain theatrical history. It's a good spot before or after the show. MasterCard and Visa only. $$$ 🍷

★★★½ **KEEN'S**—72 West 36th Street (near Avenue of the Americas)—947-3636—This stalwart midtown institution is bedecked with 19th-century playbills, theatrical posters and vintage clay pipes (belonging to former patrons like Theodore Roosevelt, General Douglas MacArthur, and George M. Cohan) racked on the ceiling. It offers hearty, honest fare which is always well prepared, plus sensible portions and friendly service. It's one of the better outposts in the vicinity of Madison Square Garden, Macy's and the Central Post Office. Curry fish chowder, Scottish smoked salmon, crab cakes, Caesar salad, prime sirloin, filet mignon au poivre, lamb chops. Hot fudge Sundae, mocha ganache cake, warm pear frangipane. $$$½ 🍷🍷🍷

★★★ **LA RÉSERVE**—4 West 49th Street (near Fifth Avenue)—247-2993—This soothing and traditional-looking French restaurant with high ceilings, warm wood paneling, comfortable banquettes and charming wildlife murals is presided over by Jean-Louis Missud, one of New York's most gracious restaurateurs. Despite the genial and serene atmosphere, slow service, and a menu that falls short of the level of creativity to which it aspires, detract from the overall impression. Nevertheless, La Réserve remains a popular spot for a business lunch or a pre-theater dinner. Foie gras with capers, grilled shrimp with linguine and red pepper coulis, roasted guinea hen in bay leaf sauce, saddle of rabbit in garlic sauce, fricassée of lobster and scallops, tarte Tatin, frozen Grand Marnier soufflé. $32 fixed price lunch, $39.50 pre-theater dinner, $54 fixed price dinner. 🍷🍷🍷

★★★½ **ORSO**—322 West 46th Street (near Eighth Avenue)—489-7212—Now celebrating its 13th season, Orso remains the most popular performance in the Theater District. Be sure to reserve in advance even for lunch. The atmosphere is unpretentious (though it gets its fair share of celebrities), service is friendly and the rustic trattoria fare is very good. Cold roasted veal in a tuna sauce with capers, house-cured salmon with red pepper mousse, pizza with pesto, tagliatelle with duck stew, white beans and tomato sauce, grilled spicy sausage with wild mushrooms and lentils, grilled sea scallops with white wine and garlic sauce, chocolate hazelnut cake. Visa and MasterCard only. $$$½ 🍷🍷

★★ **OSTERIA AL DOGE**—142 West 44th Street (between Avenue of the Americas and Broadway)—944-3643—The dramatic decor—high ceilings, soaring steel columns, period posters—is certainly grand, even if the kitchen's output is some what less magisterial. You can count on decent grilled vegetables and assorted antipasto, pleasant pasta, and very good pizza (try the Margherita with sausages and broccoli di rabe). Grilled marinated tuna, bistecca with roasted potatoes. Portions are very generous. $22.95 pre-theater dinner. $$$ 🍷🍷

🍎 ★★½ **THE RAINBOW ROOM**—30 Rockefeller Plaza

(at Rockefeller Center)—632-5000—Towering over midtown Manhattan, this dark, multi-tiered dining room with tables covered in silver lurex sports a circular dance floor with clamorous musicians decked out in ruffles and sequins. The overall effect evokes an era you may not be nostalgic for. If it's a view you are after, have a drink at the bar. If you have just come here to dine, you'll feel like a wallflower even though the ultra-talented Waldy Malouf was hired to create a menu to rival the setting. Respected for his remarkable creativity and the provenance of his ingredients, there is little evidence of his talents in the retro/contemporary selections. The staff, in their Ringling Brothers–like costumes, is harried and lacking in enthusiasm. Delays between courses can be overbearing. The wine list is very expensive and lacks balance. Best bet is to stick with throwback dishes like oysters Rockefeller, grilled lamb chops, lobster thermidor, baked Alaska. Music charge $20 per person. $$$$$ 🍷🍷

⏱ ★½ **SARDI'S**—234 West 44th Street (near Broadway)—221-8440—This legendary Broadway restaurant, where opening nights were traditionally celebrated, has been spruced up and is back in the hands of the ebullient Vincent Sardi, who still knows how to show a crowd a good time. The menu is somewhat old-fashioned, but some of the offerings such as Maryland crab cakes with basil mayonnaise or oven roasted grouper and asparagus risotto are fresher than ever thanks to the introduction of light cuisine. Otherwise, go with the dishes "à la Sardi." Fixed price lunch $24.95 (Wed. and Sat.), pre-theater dinner $39.00. $$$½ 🍷

★★★★ **SEA GRILL**—19 West 49th Street (at Rockefeller Center)—332-7610—This handsome glass-enclosed room—with a front row seat on Rockefeller Center's skating rink and terrace dining under enormous umbrellas during the summer months—joined the ranks of the city's top seafood restaurants when chef Ed Brown came aboard. Brown has a knack for seafood, and he is evolving constantly in his efforts to perfect nuances of flavor. Service is friendly, but can be ponderous. Tuna with black truffle tartare topped by chervil and chives, lobster salad with couscous and "micro-magenta spinach," Maine halibut wrapped in tuna "bacon," seared diver's sea scallops with roasted garlic and bud chives, steamed mussels with Thai red curry sauce, steamed chocolate pudding with chocolate sauce, key lime pie with currant coulis, "palette" of assorted sorbets. There is an excellent wine-by-the-glass program. Pre-theater dinner $35. $$$$$ 🍷🍷🍷🍷🍷

★★★ **TORRE DI PISA**—19 West 44th Street (between Fifth Avenue and Avenue of the Americas)—398-4400—The ultimate star here is designer David Rockwell's slant on Italianate architectural detail and the fresh and imaginative palette that ties this festive mosaic together. Enormous columns, sleek banquettes and curvaceous golden chairs along with pressed velvet walls and a blue-and-white porcelain collection are all integral parts of this fanciful look. Chef John P. Greco III has created a Tuscan-inspired menu that strives to match the surroundings. Grilled calamari with pesto, roasted onion and almond soup, fried artichokes with shaved parmesan, rigatoni and Tuscan meat ragù, rosemary chicken with currants and apricots, calf's liver with soft polenta, tiramisù, gelati. Service is pleasant but not always attentive. $$$$ 🍷🍷

★★½ **UN DEUX TROIS**—123 West 44th Street (near Seventh Avenue)—354-4148—This boisterous bistro (convenient to Broadway theaters) is lively and casual, with friendly, bustling service. The tables are covered in paper and you can create your own designs with the supplied crayons. Graavlax, Caesar salad, steak tartare, ravioli à la Provençal, grilled tuna, steak fries, tarte tatin, profiteroles. $$½ 🍷🍷

★★ **VIRGIL'S REAL BARBECUE**—152 West 44th Street (between Sixth and Seventh Avenues)—921-9494—You know you're in for some serious barbecue when the waiter hands you a terry towel instead of a napkin! In fact, Virgil's brings a compendium of the country's best barbecue recipes to a comfortable, casual and kitschy spot (if you can handle the cigarette smoke, the bar room is most fun). Stuffed jalapeno peppers, hush puppies, Texas links, Memphis pulled pork, Kansas City fried chicken, pulled Owensboro lamb, flat dogs, peanut butter pie, butterscotch pie, banana pudding. Extraordinary beer list of over 80 entries includes one of our fiery favorites, Cave Creek Chili beer. $$ 🍷🍷🍷

⏰ ★★ **WORLD YACHT CRUISES**—Pier 81 (at West 41st Street and 12th Avenue)—630-8100—Nothing quite so special exists anywhere in the city, for the three-hour yacht cruise around Manhattan gives you more spectacle than Windows on the World, The River Café and The Rainbow Room combined. Add to this some above-average continental cuisine, dancing to a good band, and gratuities (but not drinks) all for $70.47 ($83.46 on Saturdays) tax included. 🍷

★★★ **ZEN PALATE**—663 Ninth Avenue (entrance on 46th Street)—582-1669—Not only is this a smart-looking place with ochre walls, cloud-painted ceiling, and wicker café chairs, but the vegetarian food also lives up to the decor. And because there are a number of fried items here, you should get enough fat in your meal to satisfy your appetite. Moo-Shu basil rolls, "Dream Land" spinach linguine, sesame chips, sweet and sour pecans, steamed dumplings, tofu cheesecake, banana pie. No liquor license. $$½

FIFTY-FIRST TO SIXTY-FIFTH STREET (EAST)

★★ **540 PARK**—540 Park Avenue (at 61st Street in The Regency Hotel)—759-4100—This is where the "Power Breakfast" began a decade ago, and it's always jammed by 8 AM with prominent members of the business community. At noontime and after 6 PM things aren't quite as lively in this newly decorated dining room. The menu is satisfying, but rather conventional; Caesar salad, cobb salad, tuna Niçoise and burgers. Service can be disoriented. Book well in advance for breakfast. $$$$ 🍷🍷🍷

★★★ **5757**—57 East 57th Street (between Park and Madison Avenues in the Four Seasons Hotel)—758-5700—You might expect to find the treasures of Tutankhamen lurking in this soaring space with imposing stony walls and incredibly high ceilings. Unfortunately, the cloying muzak and aggressive-but-slow service make one all too aware that, alas, we are only in a hotel dining room, albeit a very handsome one. Talented executive chef Susan Weaver's menu reads well, but often fails to deliver. Celery root soup with short rib and mushroom ravioli, lobster Caesar, Maryland crab cakes with roasted bell pepper, braised lamb shank, Manhattan-style grilled shrimp, grilled Atlantic salmon. Leave room for pastry chef Bruno Feldeisen's savory crème brûlée, pumpkin tart, blueberry cheesecake. $$$$½ 🍷🍷🍷

★★★★½ **ARCADIA**—21 East 62nd Street (near Madison Avenue)—223-2900—For over a decade, devotees of Anne Rosensweig's highly satisfying seasonal fare have flocked to this enchanting, intimate space. It is enveloped by Paul Davis' colorful mural which also salutes the four seasons. Burgundy banquettes and charming floral arrangements complete the picture. The staff is most professional and knowledgeable. Signature dishes such as the lobster club sandwich, the Arcadian Caesar salad, and corn cakes with créme fraiche and caviar reign supreme at lunch. You should also consider wining preparations like mustard-crisped crab cakes with sweet pea greens, or grilled quail on wild mushroom and foie gras pasta. Additionally, there's roasted venison with sweet potato gratin and broccoli rabe, grilled salmon with Japanese eggplant salad, roasted apple with burnt sugar custard, chocolate sharpei cake, caramelized pear tart. Fixed price $58 dinner. Enophiles should be sure to request the reserve wine list. $$$$$ 🍷🍷🍷🍷

★★★½ **ARIZONA 206**—206 East 60th Street (near Third Avenue)—838-0440—Stucco walls, blanched-wood tables and floors create a casual ambience that belies the fact this is a serious destination for sophisticated Southwestern fare. (Beware the potentially piercing New York noise levels.) Chef Miles Angelo's menu is highly seasoned and creative. Santa Fe vegetable roll, shrimp and shiitake taquitas, rabbit tamale, New Mexican Niçoise salad with coriander-crusted tuna, grilled culotte steak with pasilla pesto, smoked chile-rubbed venison, molten Aztec chocolate truffle cake, caramelized banana tart. (In the adjacent Arizona Café, you can sample similar fare for much less.) $$$$ 🍷🍷

★★★★★ **AUREOLE**—34 East 61st Street (near Madison Avenue)—319-1660—With its plush upholstered walls, bas-relief designs, flattering lighting, opulent and abundant floral creations, this destination is unique. (There's also an enchanting garden for alfresco dining when weather permits.) Chef/owner Charlie Palmer is a towering presence on the national restaurant scene, and has had enormous influence on American cuisine. His staff is discreet and efficient yet enthusiastic. Oak-smoked salmon, seared foie gras escalope with rhubarb confiture, hand-cut bluefin tuna tartare, bal-

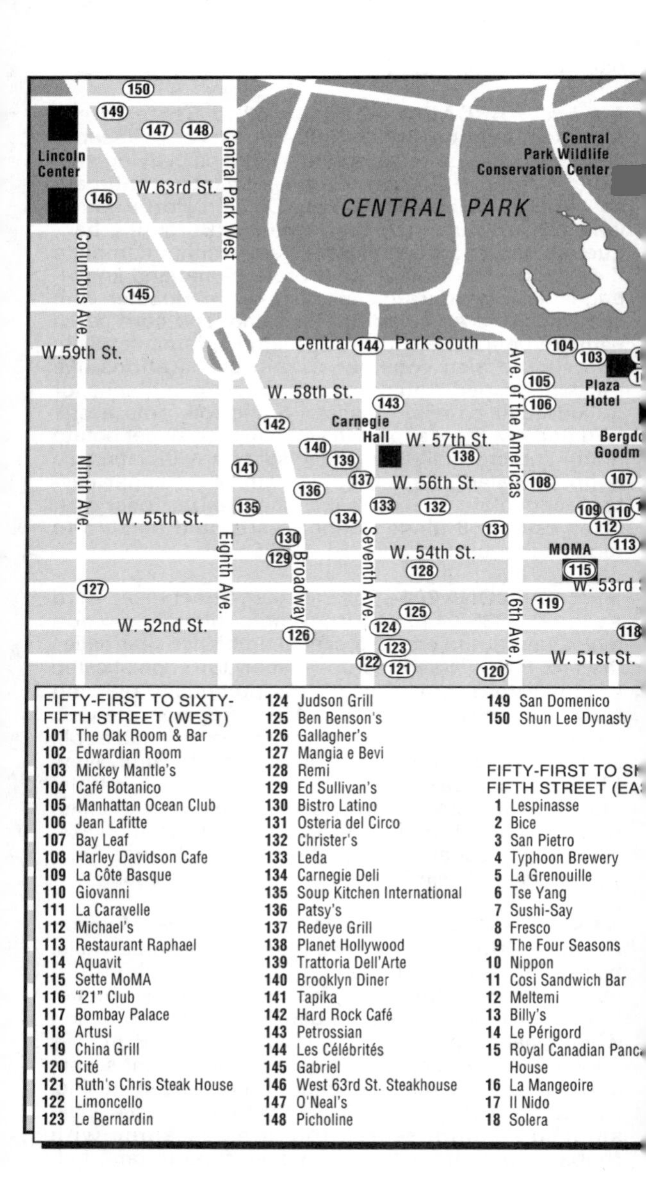

FIFTY-FIRST TO SIXTY-FIFTH STREET (WEST)

101 The Oak Room & Bar
102 Edwardian Room
103 Mickey Mantle's
104 Café Botanico
105 Manhattan Ocean Club
106 Jean Lafitte
107 Bay Leaf
108 Harley Davidson Cafe
109 La Côte Basque
110 Giovanni
111 La Caravelle
112 Michael's
113 Restaurant Raphael
114 Aquavit
115 Sette MoMA
116 "21" Club
117 Bombay Palace
118 Artusi
119 China Grill
120 Cité
121 Ruth's Chris Steak House
122 Limoncello
123 Le Bernardin
124 Judson Grill
125 Ben Benson's
126 Gallagher's
127 Mangia e Bevi
128 Remi
129 Ed Sullivan's
130 Bistro Latino
131 Osteria del Circo
132 Christer's
133 Leda
134 Carnegie Deli
135 Soup Kitchen International
136 Patsy's
137 Redeye Grill
138 Planet Hollywood
139 Trattoria Dell'Arte
140 Brooklyn Diner
141 Tapika
142 Hard Rock Café
143 Petrossian
144 Les Célébrités
145 Gabriel
146 West 63rd St. Steakhouse
147 O'Neal's
148 Picholine
149 San Domenico
150 Shun Lee Dynasty

FIFTY-FIRST TO S
FIFTH STREET (EA

1 Lespinasse
2 Bice
3 San Pietro
4 Typhoon Brewery
5 La Grenouille
6 Tse Yang
7 Sushi-Say
8 Fresco
9 The Four Seasons
10 Nippon
11 Cosi Sandwich Bar
12 Meltemi
13 Billy's
14 Le Périgord
15 Royal Canadian Panc
House
16 La Mangeoire
17 Il Nido
18 Solera

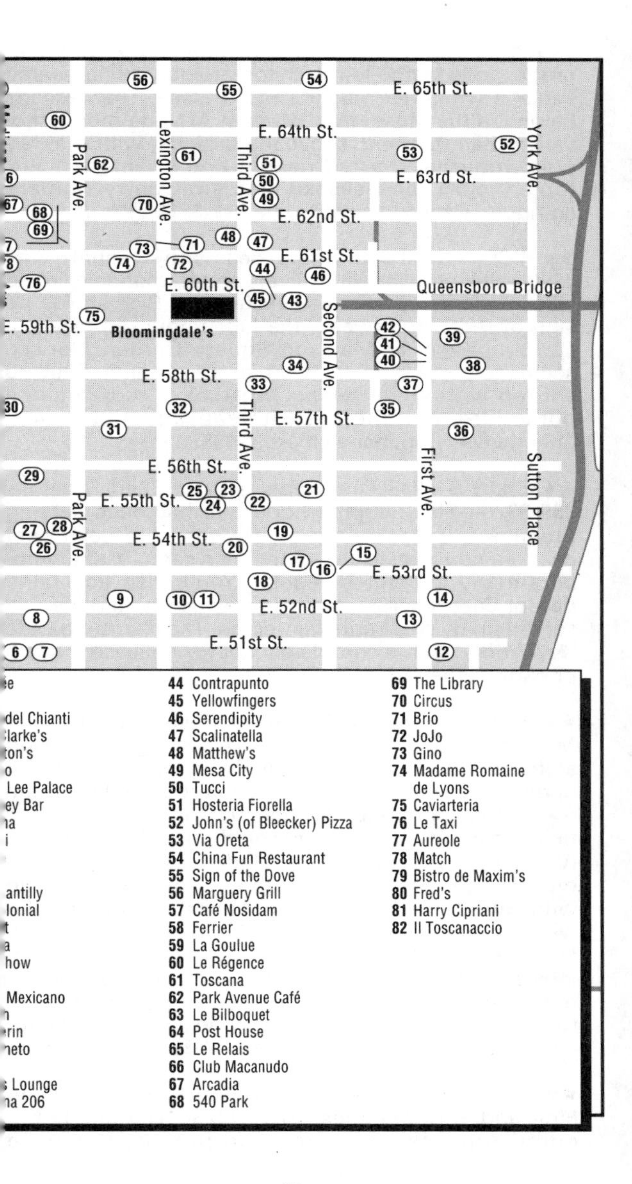

E. 65th St.
E. 64th St.
E. 63rd St.
E. 62nd St.
E. 61st St.
E. 60th St.
E. 59th St.
E. 58th St.
E. 57th St.
E. 56th St.
E. 55th St.
E. 54th St.
E. 53rd St.
E. 52nd St.
E. 51st St.
Park Ave.
Lexington Ave.
Third Ave.
Second Ave.
First Ave.
York Ave.
Sutton Place
Queensboro Bridge
Bloomingdale's
del Chianti
Lee Palace
ey Bar
antilly
lonial
Mexicano
Lounge
44 Contrapunto
45 Yellowfingers
46 Serendipity
47 Scalinatella
48 Matthew's
49 Mesa City
50 Tucci
51 Hosteria Fiorella
52 John's (of Bleecker) Pizza
53 Via Oreta
54 China Fun Restaurant
55 Sign of the Dove
56 Marguery Grill
57 Café Nosidam
58 Ferrier
59 La Goulue
60 Le Régence
61 Toscana
62 Park Avenue Café
63 Le Bilboquet
64 Post House
65 Le Relais
66 Club Macanudo
67 Arcadia
68 540 Park
69 The Library
70 Circus
71 Brio
72 JoJo
73 Gino
74 Madame Romaine de Lyons
75 Caviarteria
76 Le Taxi
77 Aureole
78 Match
79 Bistro de Maxim's
80 Fred's
81 Harry Cipriani
82 Il Toscanaccio

samic-basted mahi mahi with blood orange vinaigrette, grilled lamb loin with tomato quesadilla, seared venison with wild mushroom fricassee. The desserts belong in the Museum of Modern Art, one more innovative than the next: chocolate pudding with mascarpone mousse, roasted peanut and praline fantasy, topiary citrus cheesecake with strawberry rhubarb compote. Well-conceived wine list. $$$$ 🍷🍷🍷🍷

★★ **BICE**—7 East 54th Street (near Fifth Avenue)—688-1999—Still popular with a lively and fashionable crowd who made it a destination restaurant, Bice shows no sign of receding. Indeed, the lunch-hour din recalls a sporting event at Madison Square Garden. Service seems to depend on the whim of the evening. Sautéed shrimp with white beans, crostino di mozzarella e pomodoro, maccheroni with sausage and fennel, grilled veal chop, baby chicken. $$$$$ 🍷🍷🍷🍷

★★ **BILLY'S**—948 First Avenue (near 52nd Street)—355-8920—This neighborhood pub has been serving up seafood, steaks, chops, burgers and corn beef hash—a house specialty—for over a century, and numbers many a devoted regular. You'll also find fairly decent Caesar salad, steak tartare and onion rings—all served up by cosseting waitresses. The charming Olde New York decor is completely apt for a pleasant lunch or early dinner. $$ 🍷

★★★ **BISTRO DE MAXIM'S**—21 East 61st Street (at Madison Avenue)—980-6988—This spot has coasted along for years through several changes of chef, but under executive chef David Ruggiero's guidance, the menu has been much enlivened. Only the somewhat tired art nouveau trappings could do with a touch-up. (Window seats overlooking Madison Avenue are the most sought-after.) White bean and country ham soup with Swiss chard, peppered seared tuna carpaccio with Niçoise pasta salad, grilled spiced shrimp with cumin-scented couscous and carmoula vinaigrette, lobster risotto with fresh herbs and truffle oil, grilled marinated paillard of chicken, mezze rigate with tomatoes ("simple cuisine" for the calorie conscious), warm chocolate soufflé cake, tarte tatin. $$$$ 🍷🍷🍷

★★★★ **BOUTERIN**—420 East 59th Street (between First and York Avenues)—758-0323—The highly talented Antoine Bouterin, who presided over Le

Périgord's kitchen for years, has created an informal Provençal dining room in a large space overlooking the 59th Street bridge. Decorative pottery and pastoral knick-knacks accent a pleasing and original rustic menu. Paté maison with fresh onion jam, duck rilettes with croutons, grilled portobello mushrooms, ratatouille omelette, filet of codfish with Provençal sauce, old-fashioned roasted chicken, marquise of chocolate with strawberries, crème caramel à l'orange, country-style apple tart. Fixed price lunch is a bargain at $26. $$$$ 🍷🍷🍷

★★ **BRIO**—786 Lexington Avenue (at 61st Street)—980-2300—A tiny trattoria with warm woods, terra-cotta floors, rattan chairs and dramatic triangular light fixtures. It offers reasonably priced and uncomplicated fare such as polenta with mushrooms, white bean soup, fried artichokes, spaghetti with clams, chicken with sausage, grilled lamb chops, cheesecake, tartuffo. Service is efficient. This is the kind of place where one would feel comfortable dining alone. $$$ 🍷🍷

★★½ **CAFÉ NOSIDAM**—768 Madison Avenue (between 65th and 66th Streets)—717-5633—Forget the caper that Nosidam is Madison spelled backwards. This is a cheery place with sidewalk dining in summer that offers a serious menu. Treneto pesto, panini, bocconcini with prosciutto, spaghetti with fresh tomatoes and garlic, orecchiette with zucchini and tomatoes, ravioli with ricotta and spinach in a walnut sauce, grilled black Angus beef in barolo sauce, grilled swordfish. $$$ 🍷🍷 Fixed price $19.95 meal from noon until 7:00 PM.

★★★ **CAVIARTERIA**—502 Park Avenue (at 59th Street)—759-7410—Here's a tiny take-out shop and sandwich bar operated by New York's famed caviar emporium, perfect for splurging $96 on a three-ounce sampler of beluga, oscetra and sevruga. But for a fraction of the price, you can also have an open faced Norwegian baby shrimp sandwich, or a smoked salmon club sandwich with wild boar. Order a flute of Taittinger, and you've got the ideal venue for celebrating a major acquisition at nearby Christie's. $$$ 🍷

★★★ **CELLINI**—65 East 54th Street (between Madison and Park Avenues)—751-1555—An inviting two-story trattoria with yellow-sponged walls, festive persimmon banners draping the ceiling (which have alleviated an earlier decibel problem) and an overall country feeling—lots of pottery, woods and baskets. Cellini is presided over by Dino Arpaia, whose father successfully operated Lello at the same location for years. Polenta crostini, baked clams, fried calamari, beet-filled ravioli in gorgonzola sauce, grilled salmon with leeks, pounded veal chop, cheese cake, apple tart. Ideal for a business lunch. $$$$ 🍷🍷

★★★½ **CHARLTON'S**—922 Third Avenue (between 55th and 56th Streets)—688-4646—Discreetly positioned behind a facade of wooden blinds is this long and handsome space with a tiled floor, crisp white tablecloths and prints of old New York. Sleek and contemporary looking, it nonetheless serves up traditional steakhouse fare: Chesapeake crabcakes with roasted pepper sauce, Caesar salad, jumbo shrimp sautéed with garlic, prime aged New York sirloin, double cut Colorado lamb chops, pan-roasted Atlantic salmon, fried onion rings, apple pandowdy, flourless chocolate cake. It's an ideal spot for a business lunch. $$$½ 🍷🍷🍷

★★★ **CHINA FUN RESTAURANT**—1239 Second Avenue (corner 65th Street)—752-0810—This sweeping space serves up a highly ambitious menu, written in Chinese and English. Traditional dishes like pork dumplings, egg rolls, General Tso's chicken, orange flavor beef, sweet and sour pork are all delectably prepared. What's more, there are refreshing entries such as pan fried radish cake, Chinese sausage bun, sticky rice wrapped in lotus leaves stuffed with bean paste, sliced breast of chicken in curry sauce, beef and vegetables sautéed in Sa-chia sauce, Chinese sausage fried rice. $$ 🍷

★★★ **CIRCUS**—808 Lexington Avenue (between 62nd and 63rd Streets)—223-2566—Colorful prints of acrobats, clowns and circus animals dot the walls of this cheery Brazilian restaurant with striped upholstered chairs and a chic little bar up front draped in navy and gold. Service is low-key but attentive. Crabcakes with malagueta sauce, chicken empanada, black bean soup, chicken with saffron and okra, tuna with hearts of palm, grilled sirloin with onions and beans farofa, feijoada (Brazil's national dish, served Saturday and Sunday), carmelized bananas with vanilla ice cream, coconut mousse. $$$ 🍷🍷

★★½ **CLUB MACANUDO**—26 East 63rd Street (between Madison and Park Avenues)—752-8200—If it weren't for the cigar smoke, this would be a food-friendly restaurant. Chef Bette Publiker prepares a variety of appealing dishes ranging from shrimp won ton to fried calamari with lime-curry mayonnaise and spicy marinara sauce to an assortment of sandwiches: grilled chicken, roast pork, filet mignon and Cuban. Her menu is far more than a backdrop to this handsome cigar bar, with faux marble and faux wood accents, an authentic cigar store Indian and period prints. Calm at lunch time, the place is packed from 6:00 PM to 2:00 AM. Patrons keep their own stash of smokes in individual humidors. $$$ 🍷🍷

★★ **CONTRAPUNTO**—200 East 60th Street (near Third Avenue)—751-8616—A winning combination of bright, modern decor and a great view overlooking the bustle on Third Avenue across the street from Bloomingdale's makes Contrapunto an ideal people-watching spot. It also has some exceptional pastas like ravioli with braised beef in tomato broth, tagliarini with pancetta, tomatoes, jalapeño and parmesan, and solid main courses. End off with a slice of chocolate torte, a cup of espresso, and you have a perfectly nice lunch or a dinner before going to the movies. $$$ 🍷🍷

★★ **COSI SANDWICH BAR**—165 East 52nd Street (between Lexington and Third Avenues)—We love this concept, which originated in Paris and travels well. Cosí is a long and narrow space where you can dine in or take out. You test your creativity by specifying an array of fresh ingredients to fill their signature hearth-fired flatbread. Combine the likes of pesto-grilled chicken, roast beef or salami with everything from roasted peppers to coriander-roasted tomatoes to personalize your sandwich. Add a salad or soup of the day plus rich desserts like cheesecake and crème brûlée to make a most satisfying meal. No liquor license. $½

★★★★ **DAWAT**—210 East 58th Street (near Third Avenue)—355-7555—This most attractive space specializes in authentic and unusual regional Indian dishes. First-timers should sample assorted appetizers from "Madhur Jaffrey's Snack Cart" and such signature dishes as chicken tikka masala or tandoori shrimp or lamb vindaloo. Consider also tikkiyas—curry leaf-flavored potato cakes, sindi karhi—vegetarian stew seasoned with tamarind and fenugreek seeds, taridar chukandar, cumin flavored beets, murgh jehangiri, chicken marinated in yogurt with chili-coriander sauce, basmati rice with vegetable pilaf, plus a tantalizing array of nan and paratha. Try the Taj Mahal beer. $12.95–$13.95 fixed price lunches. $$½ 🍷

★★½ **DENIZ**—400 East 57th Street (between First Avenue and Sutton Place)—486-2255—Pale green walls, navy striped banquettes, stone floors and columns create a decorous backdrop for this unpretentious Mediterranean grill with a Turkish twist. Service is easygoing and the atmosphere is relaxed. Char-grilled mashed eggplant salad, pan-fried filo dough stuffed with feta cheese, tarama salata, shrimp casserole, grilled breast of chicken with mushrooms, grilled baby lamb-chops, Turkish pastries. $$$ 🍷🍷

★★½ **EROS**—1076 First Avenue (between 58th and 59th Street)—223-2322—It's a toss-up whether the overall effect here is more erotic or eccentric; it is certainly unexpected. The premises are illuminated almost entirely by candlelight, and around each table, there are silver-upholstered sofas that glow exotically. The Greek/Mediterranean menu is more satisfying than suggestive, with offerings like stuffed grape leaves, grilled octopus, mussels in spicy tomato sauce, shoulder of baby lamb, filet of mullet with stewed okra, moussaka, lemon yogurt cake, Greek custard in phyllo.

★★★★★ **FELIDIA**—243 East 58th Street (near Second Avenue)—758-1479—Under the discerning eye of the supremely-talented Lidia Bastianich and her husband Felice, this stuccoed and brick-walled space—with dark woods, tapestries and abundant displays of flowers—continues to excel. There is an excitement and bustle to these homey rooms (we prefer sitting downstairs), particularly at night. From the sensational pastas to the original "Tre Venezie" desserts, Felidia boasts creative and refined Italian cuisine, matched by a spectacular wine list under the supervision of Amgad Wahba. Parmesan cheese flan with truffle essence, homemade cotechino sausage with lentils, tortellacci stuffed with nettles and herbs, krafi all'Istriana ("pillows" filled with fontina, asiago and parmesan cheese, plus citrus rind, raisins and rum), roasted baby pheasant with spinach, butterflied and breaded veal chop fried with buffalo mozzarella, pan-browned salmon with chive mustard sauce, apple strudel with cinnamon ice cream, warm apricot, blueberry and frangiapane tart with apricot ice cream, fried cream lozenges with caramelized fruit. $$$$½ 🍷🍷🍷🍷🍷

★★★ **FERRIER**—29 East 65th Street (near Madison Avenue)—772-9000—A bustling and good-looking bistro (with sidewalk dining in season) which boasts a contented following (at night, decibels can be overbearing.) The menu incorporates traditional bistro fare like frisée salad, Mediterranean paté and steak tartare, along with popular American borrowings such as Maryland crab cakes and the Ferrier club sandwich. Satisfying staples include poulet Basquaise, steak frites, gigot d'agneau, crème brûlée, tarte Tatin and profiteroles. Creative wine list. Take out and free delivery within the neighborhood. Fixed price lunch and pre-theater dinner $19.97. $$$ 🍷🍷🍷

🍎 ★★★★★ **THE FOUR SEASONS**—99 East 52nd Street (between Lexington and Park Avenues)—754-9494—For more than three decades, this has been one of the most majestic and influential restaurants in New York. Its location in the Mies Van der Rohe–designed Seagram Building and its timeless Philip Johnson interior have given it actual landmark status, replete with a Picasso tapestry, paintings by Stella and Rosenquist, and a reflecting pool in the main dining room. The Grill Room is the original "power lunch" spot, but it is also a great bargain for dinner. The Four Seasons pioneered New American Cuisine, was one of the first restaurants to champion American wines and created Spa Cuisine. The restaurant is now owned by Seagram's and managed by Alex von Bidder and Julian Niccolini, whose professionalism is incomparable. Chef Christian Albin's commitment to the finest foods is as resolute as ever. Though à la carte prices are high, with some entrées $40 and more, you are getting a grandeur not matched anywhere else in New York. Macadamia-crusted tuna, smoked lobster chowder, the signature crisp shrimp with mustard fruits, crab meat cakes with crisp beets, breast of pheasant with celery root purée, venison in wild berry sauce, Four Season's fancy cake, walnut brittle, chocolate velvet cake. $$$$$ 🍷🍷🍷🍷🍷

★★½ **FRED'S**—10 East 61st Street (near Madison Avenue in Barney's basement)—833-2200—After much internal commotion, Mad.61 has been reborn as Fred's (in honor of the late Fred Pressman, chairman of Barneys), and Pino Luongo's team has been replaced by Mark Straussman's (who also owns Campagna). The talented Straussman has transformed the predominately Italian menu into a virtual smorgasbord that suits every possible craving. In its diversity, the menu doesn't always deliver, although the staff is as genial and professional as ever. Skip the signature Fred's salad (a bland concoction of canned Italian tuna and tomatoes). Do try the pizza robiola. Consider the grilled wild mushrooms, certified Angus burger, lobster salad, risotto with fennel and arugula, grilled poussin with broccoli rabe, chocolate mascarpone cake, profiteroles. Reserve well in advance for lunch. $$$½ 🍷🍷

★★★½ **FRESCO**—34 East 52nd Street (near Park Avenue)—935-3434—This bright and upbeat interior, distinguished by a dramatic mural, is presided over by the affable Scotto family. Chef Vincent Scotto's preparations are both generous and satisfying, making this an ideal spot for a business lunch. Consider the ravioli Fresco (which changes daily) or the grilled pizza (which changes weekly). Caesar salad, eggplant torta, salmon and potato crostata, pan-seared filet of Arctic char, grilled shrimp with stewed lentils, grilled double pork chop, chocolate hazelnut meringue with chocolate zabaglione, frollino with peach and zabaglione of mascarpone cheeses. $$$$ 🍷🍷🍷

★★½ **GINO**—780 Lexington Avenue (at 61st Street)—223-9658—For 52 years, Gino's has been a Lexington Avenue fixture. Its Southern Italian cuisine (and a wine list with more cocktails than Chianti) is a delightful throwback, along with its classic Scalamandre zebra-patterned wallpaper. Linoleum floors, wooden chairs and white tablecloths complete the look. The greeting is warm, and the service very old school. It's no surprise that Gino's boasts a crowd of faithful New Yorkers who swear by it. This is a great place for outings with family or friends. For many, Saturday lunch here is a tradition. Antipasti, baked clams, lentil soup, ravioli, manicotti, spaghetti with tomato and basil, tiramisù, cheesecake. No reservations, no credit cards. $$$ 🍷

★★★½ **HARRY CIPRIANI**—781 Fifth Avenue (at 59th Street in the Sherry-Netherlands Hotel)—753-5566—

The Cipriani family draws faithful customers with the same regularity it does at its legendary Venice outpost, Harry's Bar. The place rings with laughter and foreign accents, short graying men in tight suits, and gorgeous tall women in tighter skirts. The food is simple and delicious but very expensive. Service is affable but can be rushed, and newcomers may be treated with indifference. Tagliatelle verde gratinata, risotto primavera, marinated salmon with curried scallops and white beans, zucchini fritters, crêpes à la crème. $$$$$ 🍷🍷

★★½ **HOSTERIA FIORELLA**—1081 Third Avenue (between 63rd and 64th Streets)—838-7570—A fun spot that features an eclectic array of Italian specialties served up in a zany, semi-nautical interior. The superb antipasti platter is practically a meal in itself, as are the exceptional pizzas (try the Fantasia with radicchio, pesto, basil, tomatoes and pepperoni), eggless Caesar salad with shrimp, enticing foccacia sandwiches like grilled chicken with roasted peppers, cantale cheese and zucchini, good pastas, and of course, bountiful seafood. $$½ 🍷🍷

★★★★ **IL NIDO**—251 East 53rd Street (near Second Avenue)—753-8450—Back in the 1970s, Il Nido broke new ground as a serious, very authentic northern Italian restaurant surrounded by a sea of red-sauce eateries. Still going strong a quarter century later, it enjoys a loyal following. Owner Adi Giovanetti is as solicitous as can be. Even the interior decor, with its comfortable, clubby motif, has weathered well. Prices on the other hand, are extremely high, and one feels a bit apprehensive about endorsing $24 pastas or a $32 red snapper served without a single potato or vegetable. Moreover, the kitchen seems to favor traditional preparations, with few concessions to modern cucina Italiana—although the wine list does contain many contemporary bottlings. Grilled portobello mushrooms, ravioli malfatti, chicken with peppers and sausage, veal with shiitake mushrooms, torrone gelato, apple tart. $$$$$ 🍷🍷🍷🍷

★★★ **IL TOSCANACCIO**—7 East 59th Street (between Fifth and Madison Avenues)—935-3535—Another popular outpost of the Pino Luongo group which is overseen by its energetic co-owner, Cesare Dell'Aguzzo. This long and vibrant room, done up in vivid yellow and red hues with potted greenery, is packed at lunch with business diners. Chef Gianmarco Francescone's menu is a homage to Tuscan traditions. Wild mushroom ragoût, fried meatballs with cabbage and pancetta, grilled calamari, pumpkin ravioli with butter and sage, roasted boneless saddle of rabbit with broccoli rabe, Tuscan seafood stew, persimmon torte, warm apple pie. $$$ 🍷🍷🍷

★★½ **IL VIGNETO**—1068 First Avenue (at 58th Street)—755-6875—This small trattoria with terra-cotta floors, scenic murals and tiles remains home to some of the best bargains in Manhattan, starting with a fixed price lunch at $8.95. The menu has a Southern Italian bias and portions are generous. Caesar salad, baked clams, rigatoni with sausage, pancetta cream and parmesan, vitello Francese, penne with eggplant and tomato sauce, chicken with eggplant, prosciutto, mozzarella and mushrooms. Tiramisù, tartufo. $$½ 🍷🍷

★★½ **JOHN'S (of Bleecker) PIZZA**—408 East 64th Street (near York Avenue)—935-2895—Though the decor is unglamorous (glorified cafeteria status at best) this branch of the classic Bleecker Street pizza parlor (q.v.) churns out some of the best brick oven pizza and calzone on the Upper East Side. Take-out too. $½ 🍷

★★★★½ **JOJO**—160 East 64th Street (near Lexington Avenue)—223-5656—With its warm yellow walls, comfy banquettes and animated crowd, this bistro not only looks attractive, but also offers one of the most sophisticated menus around. Chef/owner Jean-Georges Vongerichten is renowned for his creative use of oils and infusions and the occasional Pacific Rim borrowing. (The talented Vongerichten also owns the nearby Thai restaurant, Vong, q.v. and the brand new Jean-Georges at Columbus Circle.) Goat cheese and potato terrine, "27" vegetables, tuna roll, sweetbreads with sliced chestnuts, porcini tart with walnut onion spread, shrimp with artichoke and basil, sauteed cod, loin of lamb with black trumpet crust, medallions of venison, chocolate Valrhona cake, poached pear on baked frangipane, apple confit with green apple sorbet. Lunch menu $25. Tasting menu $55. $$$$ 🍷🍷🍷

★★½ **JUBILÉE**—347 East 54th Street (between Second and Third Avenues)—888-3569—A comfortable, crowded and boisterous neighborhood bistro which has already developed a strong following. The traditional menu can be inconsistent. Bouillabaisse, warm goat cheese on roasted tomatoes with balsamic vinaigrette, asparagus in puff pastry with tarragon sauce, ravioli stuffed with duck confit and mushrooms, roast breast of chicken, steak frites, beef bourguignon. Crème brûlée. $$$ 🍷🍷

★★ **L'ARDOISE**—1207 First Avenue (between 65th and 66th Streets)—744-4752—This is a simple, tiny space with a no-nonsense decor: sponged walls, gray tile floors and formica tables. Service is friendly and fun. It's a perfect hideaway for an inexpensive ($7.50) lunch of onion soup, a frisée salad and an omelette or terrific à la carte items like mussels in white wine sauce. Fixed price dinner—which includes a soup du jour, the likes of blanc de volaille au foie gras, and dessert—is $25.50. $$½ 🍷🍷

★★★★ **LA GOULUE**—746 Madison Avenue (between 64th and 65th Streets)—988-8169—With its splendid turn-of-the-century paneling, lace curtains, and red leather banquettes filled with beautiful faces, this is about as close as New York comes to a chic Parisian brasserie. But it's not just a pretty place, thanks to the talents of chef Philippe Schmit and the savvy team of François and Suzanne Latapie, who run the restaurant with great style and flair. Schmit prepares such appealing fare such as wild mushroom raviolis in minestrone broth, carpaccio of tuna with lemongrass, flash-cooked salmon with tapenade, grilled chicken breast salad, steak and glorious frites. He has even refined La Goulue's signature cheese soufflé with the addition of parmesan shavings and truffle oil. Great profiteroles, tarte tatin, cappuccino mousse. Creative, constantly-evolving wine list. $$$ 🍷🍷🍷

★★★★ **LA GRENOUILLE**—3 East 52nd Street (near Fifth Avenue)—752-1495—With its stunning floral arrangements, red velvet banquettes, sconces, mirrors, and soft silk wall-coverings, La Grenouille is arguably the most romantic restaurant in New York, a reminder of a bygone style that once characterized the city's dining experience. Its menu is also quite old-fashioned. Yet the Masson family's dedication to classic perfectionism (they have presided over La Grenouille for over a quarter century) brings new meaning to such traditional fare as hors d'hoeuvres variés, ouef en gelée, snapper à la nage safroneé, poached chicken with horseradish sauce, and crevettes gratinée with lemon sabayon. Luscious desserts include plum tart, lemon meringue pie and sorbets. Service is model, especially when you are seated in the front room. The wine list is wildly expensive, as are the fixed price menus (which abound with supplements). Fixed price lunch $43; fixed price $77 dinner. Closed Monday. 🍷🍷🍷🍷

★★★½ **LA MANGEOIRE**—1008 Second Avenue (at 53rd Street)—759-7086—Gérard Donato presides over this quaint midtown bistro with its rustic Provençal touches. La Mangeoire attracts a loyal crowd who come here for Mediterranean fare. Tomato soup with onion and crab meat, caramelized onion tart, poached salmon, wild mushroom risotto, herb grilled shrimp with mint tabouleh, grilled grouper, lapin Provençal, peach tart, refreshing sorbets. $$$ 🍷🍷🍷

★★½ **LE BILBOQUET**—25 East 63rd Street (near Madison Avenue)—751-3036—Philippe Belgrange's fashionable patrons still line the streets to get a table at lunchtime. Once inside, the decor is very inviting, and the atmosphere redolent of Paris's Rive Gauche. Bilboquet's preparations are simple, but exceedingly well executed. Salad niçoise, chèvre chaud aux lardons, grilled tuna, breast of chicken. No reservations. $$½ 🍷

★★★★ **LE CHANTILLY**—106 East 57th Street (near Park Avenue)—751-2931—Chef/owner David Ruggiero strives to please all palates and pocketbooks with his tantalizing and reasonable fixed-price menus. His formal dining room is accented with warm lighting and attractive floral arrangements. Service is highly professional. Ruggiero still offers a classical French menu with the likes of steak Bordelaise, roasted chicken and Dover sole, but the focus is one more innovative selections like beet risotto with carpaccio of beef, Napoleon of tomatoes and Maine crab meat, langoustine-stuffed capellacci, bacon-wrapped monkfish, rilettes of rabbit in phyllo. Save room for patissier Eric Girerd's spectacular desserts such as aphrodisiac of chocolate and ginger with vanilla ice cream, baby grand piano of chocolate and pistachio, cognac crème brûlée. $19.97 and $29.00 fixed price lunch; $38.00 pre-theater dinner; $55 fixed price dinner. $$$$$ 🍷🍷🍷🍷

★★½ **LE COLONIAL**—149 East 57th Street (near Lexington Avenue)—752-0808—An instant favorite for ladies' lunch and trendy dinners, Le Colonial serves up pleasant Vietnamese fare in smart surroundings replete with exotic potted palms and ceiling fans. The diet conscious can delight in grilled vegetables or chicken salad, but more flavorful offerings include shrimp, rice and lettuce rolls, grilled sliced pork with bean sprouts, shrimp wrapped sugar cane, and beef salad with lemon grass and chili. The price of popularity means problematic reservations. $$$ 🍷🍷

★★★★ **LE PÉRIGORD**—405 East 52nd Street (near First Avenue)—755-6244—A low-ceilinged dining room with peach-colored walls, which conveys a quiet, bygone elegance. The greeting from owner Georges Briguet is affable, and his staff is gracious. Chef Pascal Coudouy has blossomed here, toning down the classic formality of the menu with highly appealing rustic dishes. Crab cakes with saffron mayonnaise, grilled sweetbreads with warm bean salad, paper-thin vegetable tart with goat cheese, roasted rabbit with peas and potatoes, country-style beef stew, salmon with potato crust and red wine sauce, lemon sabayon. The wine list is extensive but expensive. Fixed price $32 lunch, $52 dinner. 🍷🍷🍷🍷

★★★½ **LE REGENCE**—37 East 64th Street (near Park Avenue in the Plaza Athénée Hotel)—606-4647—One of the best kept secrets in New York, this formal, ornate and soothing dining room, presided over by the skillful chef Marcel Agnez produces creative and satisfying French fare at surprisingly reasonable prices. The staff is highly professional. House-smoked salmon pancake with a chive and curry sauce, sautéed sea scallops with oven-dried tomato ravioli and fresh basil, roasted chicken breast with toasted pine nuts, roasted Atlantic salmon with artichoke hearts, three chocolate mousse, Anjou pear baked in chocolate bread tarte. Fixed price $22.50 lunch. $$$$ 🍷🍷🍷

★★½ **LE RELAIS**—712 Madison Avenue (near 63rd Street)—751-5108—A Madison Avenue institution for dependable bistro food and exquisite people watching—which extends to the sidewalk in season. This handsome interior is always lively and brimming with a Euro-crowd. The menu is uncomplicated and dependable. Vichyssoise, poached salmon, roasted chicken, steak tartare, steak frites, chocolate cake, floating island. $$$ 🍷🍷

★★½ **LE TAXI**—37 East 60th Street (between Park and Madison Avenues)—832-5500—Now under knowledgeable new ownership, this brightly-lit interior dotted with French posters remains a popular destination for lunch or dinner. Like many neighborhood hangouts, it can be noisy. Service bustles. The bistro fare is quite authentic, but lacks great finesse. Onion soup, artichokes sauced with basil pistou, celeri remoulade, crab cakes, sautéed calf's liver, steak tartare, chocolate mousse profiteroles, tarte tatin. $$$ 🍷🍷

★★★★★ **LESPINASSE**—2 East 55th Street (off Fifth Avenue in the St. Regis Hotel)—339-6719—This formal and opulent Louis XV-style setting—with enormous floral displays, widely set-apart tables and a surfeit of guilding—is presided over by the masterful Gray Kunz, one of America's culinary potentates. He is famed for his brilliant compositions and an ethereal balance of French technique and Pacific rim seasonings. Manager Dominique Simon (formerly of Bouley) has injected a breath of fresh air into the serious setting. Service is amiable, enthusiastic and professional. Sommelier Michael MacNeil is extremely knowledgeable and delightful in manner. Herbed risotto and mushroom fricassee, Peekytoe crabmeat with rice flake-crusted shrimp, sautéed foie gras with shallot fondue, lobster gratin, pan-seared skate with shallot vinegar capers, roasted pheasant with walnut raisin vinaigrette, seared loin and confit of rabbit in a rosemary-mustard sauce, braised short rib of beef. Cinnamon rhubarb compote, poached pear tart and chocolate ice cream, chilled quince soup and honey port wine ice cream. The $44 fixed price lunch is a good bet. Degustation menus at $76 and $95. $$$$$ 🍷🍷🍷🍷🍷

★★ **THE LIBRARY**—540 Park Avenue (corner of 61st Street in The Regency Hotel)—759-4100—Done up in reproduction antique furniture, this place is meant to evoke a plush private library, where you can order anything from savories to serious fare throughout the day. The concept generally works, although seating arrangements can prove haphazard, and the kitchen can be erratic. Roasted tomato and fennel bisque with prosciutto and mini croque monsieurs, "three sandwiches" (tea-smoked chicken salad, lobster roll and glazed meat loaf), frittata with potatoes and mushrooms, and a tart of lobster, mushroom and spinach with truffle sauce. Double chocolate pudding, pear crisp, library sundae. $$$

★★ **MADAME ROMAINE DE LYONS**—132 East 61st Street (between Lexington and Park Avenues)—759-5200—The traditions of Madame Romaine are carried on in this stark space. Omelets are still the order of the day with hundreds of selections (French bacon, olives, croutons, chicken livers, sausages, ham, and a wide array of cheeses) to choose from. Our favorites include the Cluny, Mozart and Beauvilier. There is a limited dinner menu which includes pasta, chicken, lamb chops and pastries. Amex and Diner's Club only. $$

★★★★1/2 **MARCH**—405 East 58th Street (between Sutton Place and First Avenue)—838-9393—This town house setting with its plush deco-patterned banquettes and warm woods casts a flattering glow. There is a delightful garden in season. Co-owner Joseph Scalice assures highly attentive service and also oversees a spectacular wine list. Chef/co-owner Wayne Nish's cuisine is creative yet sublimely delicate. From his signature beggar's purses (filled with caviar or lobster) to his artful creations with truffles, you feel instantly pampered. Five-spiced salmon with wild mushrooms, venison salad with quinoa pilaf, poached breast of chicken in spicy cider sauce, fricassée of lobster and sea scallops with fennel and mussels, phyllo crumble, mulled cider soup with Granny Smith apples. Fixed price dinner $59.

★★★1/2 **MARGUERY GRILL**—133 East 65th Street (between Lexington and Park Avenues)—744-2533—Owner Henry Lambert has transformed Lex, with its impractical retro menu, into an appealing contemporary restaurant. It still sports soothing pastel-colored walls and Sonia Delaunay prints. Maine salmon and crabmeat cake, chilled yellowfin tuna shashimi, sauté of Hudson Valley foie gras, wild mushroom and Swiss chard risotto, herb-crusted cod in a broth of chanterelles, leeks and potatoes, lobster and asparagus fricassée, braised lamb shank, crème brûlée, and chilled mango, mint and lime soup. Fixed price lunch $19.97. $$$1/2

★★ **MATCH**—33 East 60th Street (between Park and

Madison Avenues)—906-9173—A sibling of SoHo's popular "scene" restaurant of the same name, this uptown clone applies much the same formula to court the crowds: sparse yet striking decor, with exposed metallic pipes hanging over a colossal bar, a sprinkling of overstuffed furniture, and a diverse menu complete with a raw bar, dim sum, grilled tuna burger, seared pepper tuna, and spit-roasted poussin. $$$$ 🍷🍷

★★★★ **MATTHEW'S**—1030 Third Avenue (corner 61st Street)—838-4343—The flagship restaurant of the talented and ubiquitous Matthew Kenney (he also owns Mezze, and Monzu) comes replete with palm trees, ceiling fans and Indochine-inspired upholstery and photographs. The menu, however, borrows heavily from Mediterranean and Moroccan traditions. Dining here on spiced crab cakes, Moroccan chicken or Sicilian-style squab is a bit like taking a holiday, and the cheery staff rounds out the effect. At lunch, lighter fare such as Caesar salad, tuna tartare and Mediterranean pizza beckon. Heartier dishes include charcoal-grilled octopus with fava bean salad, hazelnut-crusted foie gras, white corn risotto with pancetta, almond-crusted salmon, coriander-crusted rabbit with green herbed risotto. Cap it off with cappuccino flan and raspberry meringue bars, banana coconut upside-down cake, crème brûlée. $$$½ 🍷🍷🍷

★★ **MELTEMI**—905 First Avenue (near 51st Street)—355-4040—White stucco walls, wooden beams and a colorful display of tiles make you feel as if you are dining in a country inn. The menu offers a good selection of cold mezze—taramasalata, feta cheese, cucumber-yogurt dip, plus hot appetizers such as spinach pie and fried zucchini with garlic spread. Choose from a variety of charcoal-grilled fish, or baked shrimp Meltemi with feta cheese and tomatoes, lamb kebob, home made pastries. $$$ 🍷🍷

★★★ **MESA CITY**—1059 Third Avenue (between 62nd and 63rd Streets)—207-1919—An uptown version of lower Fifth Avenue's highly successful Mesa Grill, also overseen over by executive chef Bobby Flay. The concept travels well, but this retro interior, replete with cowboy-imprinted banquettes, low-slung tin ceilings and murals, still comes off as a glorified cafeteria compared to the flagship. Yet in its no-frills way, Mesa City offers just what the neighborhood needs: a large, noisy bar where you can sip on a wide variety of margaritas, and a host of Bobby Flay's tantalizing American Southwest preparations. Smoked shrimp cake with tomatillo sauce, shrimp and cilantro pesto quesadilla, hot and sweet sausage quesadilla, charred red chile lamb, grilled pork chops adobo, molasses BBQ ribs, chile-rubbed chicken, Southwestern fries, ice cream sundae, rocky road chocolate pudding. $$$ 🍷🍷

★★★½ **MONKEY BAR**—60 East 54th Street (near Madison Avenue)—838-2600—This is a slick, glitzy, retro-looking space with rust-colored velvet columns and purple-hued walls. Bright gold frames are filled with black-and-white images of a Hollywood long gone by. Tiny monkeys cavort about the light fixtures and railings. The adjoining Monkey Bar, replete with its own monkey-intensive motif, is among the most popular bars in town. Monkey Bar eggless Caesar salad, BBQ spare rib salad, braised chanterelle salad, grilled stuffed squid, grilled Fundy Bay salmon, roast Amish chicken breast with potato sage pancake, sliced sirloin steak with onion rings, chocolate peanut butter bombe, cappuccino parfait. $$$$ 🍷🍷

★★½ **MR. CHOW**—324 East 57th Street (near First Avenue)—751-9030—Some diners are surprised to learn this restaurant is still prospering. In fact, the quality of the service and food improved once the novelty factor of the place died down some years ago although the kitchen's output can be inconsistent. The striking neo-Deco decor has stood up particularly well. Mr. Chow's fried dumplings, deep-fried seaweed, Peking chicken, sweet-and-sour pork, pink prawns, and fried rice. Even the prices don't seem out of line any more. $$$½ 🍷🍷🍷

★★★ **NIPPON**—155 East 52nd Street (near Lexington Avenue)—688-5941—One of the first modern Japanese restaurants in the United States, Nippon has been a pioneer in everything from interior design to introducing sushi and sashimi (still superb) to the American public, and more recently, such delicacies as usuzukuri (paper-thin marinated fluke). Goma-Ae (a medley of Zen vegetables), yamakake (raw marinated tuna), hanazukuri (marinated raw beef), tempura, shabu shabu, tonkatsu-kodonburi (pork cutlet). The restaurant is large but artfully partitioned, and the staff is cordial at lunch. At dinner, service can be languid

and indifferent. Tatami rooms for parties. $$$½ 🍷
$18.50–$28.50 fixed price lunch.

★★★★½ **OCEANA**—55 East 54th Street (near Madison Avenue)—759-5941—Chef Rick Moonen's professionalism is reflected in every morsel of his dazzling cuisine. Distinguished by a flawless sense of spicing, his menu is constantly evolving. Oceana's look has also changed with a chic, newly decorated upstairs space, replete with beautiful woods, geometric-patterned carpet and a popular bar. Downstairs evokes the mood of a smooth ocean liner. Shrimp and pork potstickers, salmon tartare wrapped with smoked salmon, Oceana East Coast bouillabaisse, tuna carpaccio with capers and asiago cheese, jumbo crabcake in chipotle sauce, mahi mahi with corn and cilantro vinaigrette, seared halibut with risotto, roast monkfish "osso buco" with saffron risotto. Desserts are better than ever thanks to pastry chef David Carmichael: mint chocolate crisp parfait, mascarpone mousse, poached pear and glazed sabayon. $34 three-course fixed price lunch. $$$$½ 🍷🍷🍷🍷

★★½ **OTABE**—68 East 56th Street (between Madison and Park Avenues)—223-7575—A highly stylized and serene setting, which features numerous Kyoto specialties along with authentic Japanese dishes like mixed oshitashi (steamed spinach, eggplant, broccoli and shiitake mushrooms) and age soba (buckwheat noodles with fried white fish.) You'll also find a broad array of traditional preparations like assorted sashimi, shrimp tempura, tazuna rolls, and kaiseki kuzushi. Alternatively, in the Teppan grill room foods are prepared at table-side. Service can be disorganized. $$$½

○★½ **P.J. CLARKE'S**—915 Third Avenue (at 55th Street)—759-1650—A throwback saloon, and one of New York's most popular at that. Once you wade past the crowd in the front room bar, (tip: enter by the side door on 55th Street and skip the throng), you'll find a pleasant dining room in back serving burgers, chile and home fried potatoes. Convenient to Third Avenue cinemas, this is a spot where history looms larger than the cuisine—which has declined marginally of late. The wait for a table can sometimes be agonizing. $$ 🍷

★★★★ **PARK AVENUE CAFE**—100 East 63rd Street (at Park Avenue)—644-1900—Marble floors, blond woods, and a whimsical collection of Americana create a smart and stylish backdrop for chef David Burke's imaginative and satisfying menus. (The adjacent Park Avenue Café Townhouse, which shares the same kitchen, caters to private parties.) The talented Burke has elevated eclectic American fare into a true art form. Don't ignore stand-bys like salmon and tuna tartare, the trademark pastrami salmon or Mrs. Ascher's steamed vegetable torte. Consider carpaccio of tuna with sea urchin mousse, black and white bean soup with shrimp and jack cheese quesadilla, shiitake hash, chicken cobb salad, Chinese-style ribs with grilled prawns, raspberry and lemon tart, milk chocolate crème brûlée, strawberry rhubarb tart with cinnamon ice cream. $$$$ 🍷🍷🍷🍷

★★★ **PELAGO**—157 East 55th Street (between Lexington and Third Avenues)—935-4321—Pelago is a welcome addition to the neighborhood. You enter via a long, inviting bar (with mountains of chips to nibble on) past a wave-like painted mural, into a second room with a domed ceiling, stained glass and watercolors dotting the walls. Chef Ian Russo delivers a focused menu with some highly creative dishes that can wow. Blackened tuna, Mediterranean cobb salad, haloumi and kasseri fondue with grilled pita. Crispy potato-wrapped trout filet is a real winner, though the veal chop with wild mushroom sticks could benefit from more time in the oven. Almond praline cheesecake, crème brûlée, hot chocolate soufflé. $$$½ 🍷🍷

★★★½ **THE POST HOUSE**—28 East 63rd Street (near Madison Avenue)—935-2888—An eclectic Americana theme is a great setting for a business lunch or a lively dinner. The original management provides continuity. The Post House remains a perfect place to dine with guests of diverse palates; you can subsist on standbys like Caesar salad, crab cakes, lobster Cobb salad, and sirloin steak, or opt for lemon pepper chicken, poached salmon with snowpeas, Cajun grilled filet mignon, filet tips. No matter what, don't overlook the addictive French fries and onion rings. And do take advantage of one of the city's finest wine lists. $$$$ 🍷🍷🍷🍷

★★★ **ROSA MEXICANO**—1063 First Avenue (near 58th Street)—753-7407—The signature pomegranate margaritas here are a perfect match for the stuccoed walls which emit a rose-colored glow. The front room boasts decorative banners and a densely-packed bar which is far more boisterous than the space in back with its twinkling star fixtures. Either way, this Josephina Howard creation is still going strong and delivers above-average Mexican fare. Service can be harried and the kitchen delivers some dishes suspiciously quickly. Guacamole prepared at tableside to individual specifications is a classic. Ceviche of bay scallops, raviolis poblanos, beef short ribs marinated in beer and lemon, crepas filled with baby shrimp and chile pasilla, enchiladas de mole poblano, fresh mango with coconut ice cream. $$½ 🍷

★★ **ROYAL CANADIAN PANCAKE HOUSE**—1004 Second Avenue (corner 53rd Street)—980-4131—Clearly not for the cholesterol and calorie conscious, this cramped, but lively space serves up every imaginable combination on the pancake and waffle circuit—over 60 varieties in all. Portions here are so large they could accommodate both a Mountie and his horse. For a twist, try a "Womlet"—a ham omelette served over a waffle. Then there's the Royal Canadian Cracker—two fried eggs and bacon over a pancake. Leave room for the barbecued mountain sausages. No liquor license. No credit cards. $½

★★★★ **SAN PIETRO**—18 East 54th Street (near Madison Avenue)—753-9015—The Bruno Brothers, who also run Sistina uptown, have made San Pietro one of the liveliest and most consistent Italian restaurants in midtown. Grilled sardines, fried zucchini, tubettini al pescatore, chickpea pasta with pesto, cotecchino with fava beans and mostarda di Cremona, risotto with white truffles, grilled sea bass, gelati and sorbetti, semifreddo. $$$$ 🍷🍷🍷

★★★½ **SCALINATELLA**—201 East 61st Street (corner Third Avenue)—207-8280—Down, down, down more than a dozen stairs and finally you are greeted by a display of baskets overflowing with fresh produce. This sub-street level space sports primitive stone walls, black contemporary chairs and shiny marble floors. Service is friendly, the portions quite generous. (Daily specials sometimes come at a premium; check the price before ordering.) Minestrone soup, beef carpaccio, grilled vegetables, farfalle with spinach, mascarpone and bacon, linguine with seafood, veal chop, semifreddo, tiramisù, gelati. $$$$ 🍷🍷

★½ **SERENDIPITY**—225 East 60th Street (near Second Ave)—838-3531—Looking as funky as when it opened in the 1960s, Serendipity is as good as its name—a swell little place where you'll find all sorts of surprises, from campy gifts, postcards and paraphernalia to some very tasty food like chili, burgers and scrumptious desserts like frozen hot chocolate. There is actually a "serious" menu too, featuring breast of chicken, grilled salmon, etc., if foot long hot dogs don't appeal. The menu is cosseting for diners of all ages. Slow service. $$

★★★★ **SHUN LEE PALACE**—155 East 55th Street (near Lexington Avenue)—371-8844—For more than a quarter of a century, Shun Lee has long been the standard by which other uptown Chinese restaurants are judged. Still basking in its recent renovation, the restaurant is presided over by the enterprising and skillful Michael Tong. The kitchen boasts unique dishes from six Chinese regions (plus a more American creation—spa cuisine), prepared under the guidance of three master chefs. The menu is more exciting than ever—though ordering à la carte can be quite expensive. Beijing fried dumplings, Szechuan wonton, orange pork, rare tuna in spicy Hunan sauce, crispy prawns with passion fruit, Chan-do chicken, profiteroles, chocolate mousse cake. $$$$ 🍷🍷🍷🍷

★★★½ **SIGN OF THE DOVE**—1110 Third Avenue (at 65th Street)—861-8080—The ornate, pastel-infused decor, replete with brick archways and classical statuary is more redolent of Palm Beach's Worth Avenue, than Manhattan's Third. Even the service seems a bit distant, if not outright indifferent. Nonetheless, talented chef Andrew D'Amico's menu helps to compensate. Grilled sea scallops with polenta, smoked salmon consommé with lobster, artichoke tortellini, herb-crusted cod, sautéed Long Island duck breast, roasted loin of venison, quince soup with pomegranate, chocolate chestnut opera cake, lemon meringue tart. Fixed price $19.97 lunch. $$$$$ 🍷🍷🍷🍷

★★★★ **SOLERA**—216 East 53rd Street (near Lexington Avenue)—644-1166—Under the talented chef Dominic Cerrone, Solera has become a destination not just for the city's finest Spanish fare, but for cuisine that is fresh and innovative. Solera's cheery interior is redolent of a country inn, and the staff is most efficient. The menu is so tantalizing, you want to order everything. Start with an array of tapas such as marinated anchovies, fried calamari, or a casserole of chorizo, wild mushrooms and snails. Be sure to include patatas bravas. Fresh shrimp with leeks and sorrel, herb-crusted monkfish, marinated and grilled butcher's steak, mango passion soup with melon, spice soufflé and warm apple compote, chocolate cherry tart. Take advantage of the wide variety of wines and sherries by the glass. $$$½ 🍷🍷🍷🍷

★★★½ **SUSHI-SAY**—38 East 51st Street (between Madison and Park)—755-1780—A plethora of blond woods define the simple decor, which is as amiable as the service. Seating is a tad cramped, but this is nonetheless a great spot to sample some of the best sushi and sashimi New York has to offer. You can tailor your sushi selection to your personal tastes by ordering from the à la carte menu, replete with yellowtail, salmon caviar, sea urchins, and California rolls—priced between $1.50 and $5.00—or sample the likes of excellent tuna tartare, futomaki rolls, (mushrooms, crab sticks, omelet, and squash) and the copious Sushi-say bento. Reservations a must. $$½ 🍷

★★½ **TAPAS LOUNGE**—1078 First Avenue (between 59th and 58th Streets)—421-8282—No matter that you are unlikely to encounter anything nearly so flamboyant or boisterous in Spain, for this lively spot (with flamenco dancing on Thursdays) is a great addition to the Manhattan late-night scene. Tapas Lounge serves up authentic and well-executed fare in surroundings redolent of a whacky medieval great room. There's a wide array of tapas to choose from: Sliced Serrano ham, chorizo and manchego cheese, shrimp poached in garlic oil, veal meatballs, mussels in green sauce, patatas bravas, fried calamari, mushroom croquettes, marinated anchovies, salt cod, cucumber and potato salad. Amex only. $$ 🍷🍷½

★★★ **TOSCANA**—843 Lexington Avenue (near 64th Street)—517-2288—This beguiling trattoria is the Bitici brothers' most recent venture. It is a small space with a compact menu, but entirely pleasing results. Shrimp salad with basil sauce, grilled portabello mushrooms, ravioli stuffed with sun dried tomato and pignoli, pansotti stuffed with ricotta in walnut sauce, pappardelle with duck sauce, grilled breast of chicken salad with baby artichokes, broiled sausages with Tuscan beans. $$$ 🍷🍷🍷

★★★ **TSE YANG**—34 East 51st Street (near Madison Avenue)—688-5447—Like its twin in Paris, this is particularly elegant and comfortable place to dine, with a soothing inerior and widely spaced apart tables. Don't expect a trailblazing menu, just well prepared, traditional specialties. Peking hot and sour shrimp, spring and autumn rolls, Tse Yang fried prawns, tangy and spicy chicken, lobster Szechuan style, sautéed roast pork, filet of beef in a tea-spiced sauce. $25.75 fixed price lunch. $$$$ 🍷

★★ **TUCCI**—206 East 63rd Street (between Third and Second Avenues)—355-6437—Behind the dark green facade is a casual and boisterous neighborhood hangout with exposed brick walls. There's a TV at the bar with a Matt Le Blanc look-alike tending drinks. The atmosphere and service are friendly and upbeat, prices are reasonable and although the food lacks finesse, it is honestly prepared and portions are huge. Minestrone soup, mussels with wine, pizza altucci, focaccie Tuccese (robiola) risotto with vegetables mushrooms and crabmeat, lasagna alla Bolognese, bass roasted in the wood-burning oven, flourless chocolate cake. $$$ 🍷🍷

★★★ **TYPHOON BREWERY**—22 East 54th Street (between Madison and Fifth Avenue)—754-9006—With its gleaming vats, brick walls, metal tabletops and geometric chairs, the space is angular and masculine in feeling, and mirrors the boisterous crowd. The Thai-inspired menu is far more sophisticated than you'd expect in such a spot. So is the copious wine and beer list, created by Steve Olson. Tasting is the route to take here, from mini-flights of beer or ale, to satays of shrimp, calamari or mushrooms. Leave room for main courses like wok-sautéed Japanese eggplant, grilled lemongrass chicken and spicy Thai fries. The banana dessert is a must. Typhoon Brewery is fun and unique. A well-trained and knowledgeable staff caps off the experience. Beware the amazing noise levels. $$$ 🍷🍷🍷🍷

★★½ **VIA ORETA**—1121 First Avenue (near 64th Street)—308-0828—A pleasant and cozy neighborhood trattoria, convenient to local cinemas. Caesar salad, zuppa di pesce, deep fried baby artichokes, crostini, stuffed peppers, penne with zucchini, capellini primavera, orrechiette with sausage and broccoli di rabe, pollo e salsiccia, scampi fra diavolo, zabaglione freddo, cheese cake. $$½ 🍷🍷

★★★★ **VONG**—200 East 54th Street (at Third Avenue)—486-9592—Chef Jean-Georges Vongerichten's spectacular homage to Thailand, where he once apprenticed, equally embraces fine French textures (he is also owner of the popular French bistro, JoJo, q.v.). The dramatic space is resplendent in gold leaf, creative wall treatments, and custom-designed lighting fixtures that are original and unexpected. The menu is innovative and ever-changing. Crab spring roll with tamarind dipping sauce, chicken and coconut milk soup, quail rubbed with Thai spices, veal chop with kumquat chutney, Muscovy duck breast with sesame sauce, grilled beef and noodles in ginger broth. Bananas in phyllo parcels, crispy rice cakes with raspberry and coconut cream, lacquered peach. $$$$ 🍷🍷🍷🍷

★★ **YELLOWFINGERS**—1009 Third Avenue (at 60th Street)—751-8615—Convenient to Bloomingdale's and perfect for a light bite after a movie. Good Caesar salad, onion rings. An enticing array of entrées ranges from sandwiches like soft shell crab with red onion and basil on sourdough to pepper crusted, pan seared tuna. Skip the burgers. Nice selection of wines by the glass. $$ 🍷🍷

★★½ **ZONA DEL CHIANTI**—1043 Second Avenue (at 55th Street)—980-8686—This entry caught on fast with the neighborhood. Chef-owner Eric Miller's Italian food has some real heft to it, though he tends to overdo the number of ingredients. Service can be slow, despite a very amiable wait staff. The room itself is beige and neutral, not unlike a café in a Florida resort. The wine list is admirably weighted with Tuscan reds and fairly tariffed, with 28 selections under $30. Fritto misto of seafood, fettuccine with veal ragù, roasted whole fish, veal chop stuffed with prosciutto and fontina. $$$ 🍷🍷

FIFTY-FIRST TO SIXTY-FIFTH STREET (WEST)

🍎 ★★★½ **"21" CLUB**—21 West 52nd Street (near Fifth Avenue)—582-7200—"21" is the grand old dame who has seen it all. An infamous speakeasy during

Prohibition, it has weathered the decades to become an integral part of American restaurant lore. With its butter colored walls, toy-festooned ceilings, red banquettes and checkered tablecloths, it remains a classic, catering primarily to NYC's moneyed elite. New chef Eric Blauberg shows great promise, but does not yet appear to be up to the task of maintaining the "21" experience. He has modified old favorites such as the "21" burger (overladen with oregano), the Caesar salad and crabcakes. New additions to the menu such as pan roasted shrimp with chorizo sausage and cracked olives, and seared moulard duck breast with quince-walnut sauce seem overly ambitious. Stick to safer bets such as fresh oysters, the salmon tasting, roasted organic chicken, black Angus ribeye. For dessert, skip the profiteroles in favor of banana bread or rice pudding. The wine cellar here is legendary, but when you consider the prices, you might pine for Prohibition days when patrons could bring their own. Service, however, is impeccable; full of personality and appropriate to the tony crowd. $$$$$ 🍷🍷🍷🍷🍷

★★★★ **AQUAVIT**—13 West 54th Street (near Fifth Avenue)—307-7311—Thanks to the arrival of chef Marcus Samuelsson, the kitchen at this former Rockefeller townhouse is rivaling the dramatic decor (towering ceilings, waterfall, multi-levels). Samuelsson has improved upon the restaurant's Scandinavian traditions by introducing more eclectic, contemporary fare. You can still delight in a herring plate, graavlax with pickled fennel, Swedish meatballs, Icelandic shrimp, Arctic venison with potato-pear strudel, sautéed atlantic salmon with sweet potato pancake, warm chocolate cake, gingerbread spice cake with mascarpone ice cream. (During game week the menu sports reindeer carpaccio and roasted boar. Also watch for Aquavit's crayfish festival.) Fixed price lunch $29, pre-theater dinner $39, three-course dinner $58. 🍷🍷🍷

★★★½ **ARTUSI**—36 West 52nd Street (between 5th Avenue and Avenue of the Americas)—582-6900—Entering this sleek and clean Milanese interior, you receive an unusually warm greeting. Chef Mauro Mafrici's creative menu, distinguished by its extraordinary range of tastes and textures, confronts you with an array of tantalizing choices. Pinzimonio of vegetables with grilled scallops, smoked arista, white lasagnetta with fresh buffalo ricotta and artichoke sauce, seared swordfish with braised onions and canellini beans, leg of rabbit roasted with honey and herbs, braised veal with carrot galette, brioche with fresh fruit and banana ice cream, meringato of chocolate hazelnut, frollino with peach and zabaglione of mascarpone. $$$$ 🍷🍷🍷

★★★½ **BAY LEAF INDIAN RESTAURANT**—49 West 56th Street (between Fifth and Sixth Avenues)—957-1818—The starkness of Bay Leaf's interior decor is more than compensated for by the elegant and refined flavors and ultra-contemporary accents of chef Walter D'Rozario's menu. Appetizers like steamed lentil cakes with mustard seeds (khaman dhokla), spicy pickled shrimp (ghinga balchao), and potato crisps with onions and bean sprouts (dahi batata poori), serve as an apt introduction. You can navigate across India with main course specialties from Madras, like chicken and curry leaves (kodi mellagu chettinad), star anise flavored lamb in saffron-almond sauce from Kashmir, or cheese and vegetable dumplings (phaldhari kofta). There are ten different breads, and a variety of sorbets. $$$ 🍷🍷

★★★½ **BEN BENSON'S**—123 West 52nd Street (near 7th Avenue)—581-8888—Has New York no end to great steak houses? Apparently not, for Ben Benson's serves marvelously rich, beefy steaks and chops, excellent seafood, wonderful crab cakes, hearty soups, and does it with aplomb and friendliness of a kind you don't always find at Ben's competitors. The place is loud, masculine, and is brightly lit. Desserts, such as bread pudding and pecan pie, have improved a great deal. Creative wine list. $$$$½ 🍷🍷🍷🍷

★★★½ **BISTRO LATINO**—1711 Broadway (overlooking 54th Street)—956-1000—Don't be put off by the second-story location, the peep show next door or the odd elevator you take up to Bistro Latino. Once inside you'll have a ball—or a tango (Wednesday) or a salsa (Saturday). But we come here for chef Rafael Palomino's (formerly of An American Place and River Café, as well as a stint at Michel Guérard) food. His creativity and respect for Caribbean (especially Cuban) traditions make his menu exciting and authentic as well. Ecuadorian seviche with plantain chips, Colombian sirloin empanadas, shrimp and coconut salad with mango, churrascos with mojo sauce spiced by garlic and thyme, Argentinean steak in chimichurri sauce, fruit flans. $$$½ 🍷🍷

★★★½ **BOMBAY PALACE**—30 West 52nd Street (near Fifth Avenue)—541-7777—Long one of NYC's premier Indian restaurants, Bombay Palace drifted into complacency, then mediocrity as the chain expanded to so many other cities. Thanks to the renewed attention of owner Iqbal Chatval, Bombay Palace has been revitalized. Service is now professional, the decor refreshed with polished dark wood and Indian antiquities, and the food better than ever, with many specialties unique to Bombay Palace. Vegetarians could feast here for days on end before running out of delicacies. Red snapper pakora, aloo tikki with peshwari red chutney, all breads, tandoori trout, lamb chops kandhari, Punjabi lamb bhuna, baby eggplant with cauliflower and potatoes, paneer and rice pulaos, ras malai, kofta. Buffet lunch at $11.95. $$$ 🍷

★★ **BROOKLYN DINER USA**—212 West 57th Street (between Seventh and Eight Avenues)—977-1959—The inspiration here is all Brooklyn: a spiffy, boxy, neon-lit diner, replete with colorful tiles, curvy woods and of course, a mural of Ebbets Field. It's great fun, friendly, and serves up nostalgic, but surprisingly satisfying fare. "15 bite" Brooklyn hot dog, Clareena's fried chicken, breadless Reuben sandwich, Avenue U roast beef, eggplant rollatini, banana split, cherry Coke, egg cream. $$ 🍷

★★★ **CAFÉ BOTANICO**—160 Central Park South (between Sixth and Seventh Avenues in the Essex House Hotel Nikko New York)—484-5120—Chef Robert Bagli presides over a cheery, pastoral setting (ideal for a business meal thanks to widely spaced apart tables). His menu is appealingly eclectic; shrimp tempura with sesame, goat cheese and vegetable brik, truffled sweetbread ravioli, roasted chicken with figs and cous cous, pizza with bresaola, tomato and basil, smoked and seared salmon with roasted beets and Yukon potatoes, roasted rack of lamb with sweet peppers and chick peas, pineapple tarte. $$$ 🍷🍷🍷🍷

★★ **CARNEGIE DELI**—854 Seventh Avenue (at 55th Street)—757-2245—Billing itself as "The World's Best," the Carnegie Deli, with its bright, neon-lit facade, boldly advertises its claim. This NYC institution—with brisk waiters and walls studded with pics of celebrity patrons—offers an enormous variety of whimsically named dishes but no frills and no credit cards. The towering sandwiches can barely fit on a plate let alone through your mouth. There's "Carnegie Haul" (a triple-decker pastrami tongue and salami combo), "Nova on Sunday" (made of smoked salmon, lake sturgeon and Bermuda onion), plus Hungarian goulash, "Julienne Child" chefs' salad, Carnegie's famous hamburger and cheesecake galore. $½

★★★ **CHINA GRILL**—52 West 53rd Street (off Avenue of the Americas)—333-7788—This handsome, kite-festooned dining room with an eclectic menu is situated in the vast ground floor of the CBS building. It began as a California transplant in the style of Wolfgang Puck's Chinois on Main, but has become very much embedded in New York dining tradition. Caesar salad with crispy wontons, broccoli rabe dumplings with roasted tomatoes, lamb dumplings with ginger mushroom sauce, Thai beef satay with soba noodles and spicy peanut sauce, crackling calamari with lime-miso dressing, Granny Smith apple cake, pumpkin cheesecake. Can be noisy. $$$ 🍷🍷🍷

★★★★ **CHRISTER'S**—145 West 55th Street (between Sixth and Seventh Avenues)—974-7224—Chef Christer Laarsson presides over a highly original Scandinavian interior, replete with plaid banquettes and whimsical fishes. The predominately seafood menu contains both classical renderings and spicy contemporary accents. Swedish graavlax with mustard dill sauce, tuna tartar with mango chutney and ginger sauce, fried oysters with pineapple salsa and cilantro, house smoked serrano salmon with black beans, and tomatillo salsa, tandoori salmon with peach chutney and vegetable curry, grilled swordfish with pesto and roasted pepper sauce. Arctic sundae, lingonberry bread pudding, lime marinated fruit. Well priced wine list. Fixed price $19.97 lunch. $$$ 🍷🍷🍷

★★★ **CITÉ**—120 West 51st Street (near Avenue of the Americas)—956-7100—A flamboyant and stylish brasserie-cum-steakhouse with a spirited and professional staff. The menu is succinct and satisfying, making this a popular midtown haunt for steaks, chops, and seafood—ideal for a business meal. Grilled corn chowder, salmon Charlotte, pan seared crab cakes, baby rack of lamb, grilled tuna with shiitakes and snow peas, filet mignon with superb French fries, Cité cheesecake, fruit crisp. There are two excellent fixed price dinners: pre-theater at $37.50; and post 8 PM with four complimentary wines at $49.50. $$$$ 🍷🍷🍷🍷

★★½ **ED SULLIVAN'S**—1697 Broadway (at 54th Street)—541-1697—Located in the building which for years was home to the Ed Sullivan Show (it's David Letterman's fiefdom now), this glitzy, two-story space with padded booths and oversize mirrors wonderfully evokes the 1950s showbiz scene with vintage photographs and paraphernalia from bygone performances. (Modern-day impresario Paul Shaffer occasionally presides over live music.) The menu is a bit of a throwback too; an eclectic and pleasing combination of Cantonese and New York steakhouse fare. It's a particularly good mix for family outings or when you are entertaining guests of diverse palates. Caesar salad, spare ribs, tuna tartare, spring rolls, hamburger, surf and turf, Peking chicken, chocolate torte, ice cream sandwich. $$$½ 🍷🍷🍷

★★★ **THE EDWARDIAN ROOM**—59th Street and Fifth Avenue (in the Plaza Hotel)—759-3000—It is hard to surpass the majestic atmosphere of this grand, turn-of-the-century dining room, with a wonderful prospect overlooking Grand Army Plaza. Although the ambiance is high Edwardian, the menu is quite contemporary, and service is attentive and friendly. Salmon tartare with curry oil, napoleon of buffalo mozzarella and ripened tomatoes, roasted rack of lamb with braised beans, seared Muscovy duck breast with corn and crispy duck salad. Pre-theater dinner is $42. $$$$$ 🍷🍷🍷🍷

★★★ **GABRIEL**—11 West 69th Street (between Broadway and Columbus)—956-4600—Here you'll find an attractive crowd in an equally attractive setting, defined by a curvy bar and banquettes, large modern paintings and Dali-esque ceiling fixtures. Sponged walls hung with mirrors open up the room. The staff is friendly and efficient. The menu is ambitious and reads like culinary poetry, but does not always live up to its prose. Spicy mussel soup, cured salmon with shaved fennel, grilled and marinated calamari, artichoke risotto, pappardelle with braised boar, rabbit legs over polenta. Banana bread pudding, chocolate pumpkin semifreddo. Be sure to order the Zagat espresso! $$$ 🍷🍷

★★★½ **GALLAGHER'S**—228 West 52nd Street (near Broadway)—245-5336—Easily the best West Side steakhouse, both for its food and unique atmosphere. The walls are covered with memorabilia of Broadway and sports legends, the waiters are affable, and the bar is convivial. You'll see huge sides of beef in the window, and what you see is what you'll get: perfectly aged and prepared steaks, chops, and side orders in big portions. The wine list is commendable though lacks depth. Tomatoes and Bermuda onion, oxtail soup, sirloin, lamb chops, mashed potatoes, chocolate mousse cake, rice pudding. $$$$ 🍷🍷

★★½ **GIOVANNI**—47 West 55th Street (between Fifth Avenue and Avenue of the Americas)—262-2828—The space that formerly housed Madeo has been effectively transformed with whimsical trompe l'oeil touches. The menu is more prosaic Italian, with occasional flashes of fantasy. Frisée with gorgonzola and pancetta, insalata mista with goat cheese and roasted tomatoes. Monkfish with caponata, risotto with porcini mushrooms, grilled veal chop with mashed potatoes, tiramisù, chocolate pecan tart. $$$½ 🍷🍷🍷

★½ **HARD ROCK CAFE**—221 West 57th (near Broadway)—459-9320—People don't come here for dinner or lunch as much as they do for a lift. Decor aptly consists of a guitar collection belonging to celebrated musicians. Music blares from noon until the wee hours. The crowd is very young, birthday parties are being celebrated constantly, and don't leave without buying a t-shirt or two for your niece in Des Moines. Good burgers and sandwiches. Skip the pork barbecue. $½ 🍷

★★ **HARLEY DAVIDSON CAFE**—1370 Avenue of the Americas (at 56th Street)—245-6000—With rock music and a litany of fantastic Harleys on display (including one belonging to Billy Joel, and another from the set of "Easy Rider"), who cares if the sesame crusted catfish is overcooked? Here's a menu that combines burgers, (chili) fries, sandwiches and pasta with an attempt at more serious fare such as blackened cajun chicken, Carolina pulled pork, Mississippi mud pie, and triple chocolate dessert. There are amusing cocktails like the aptly named Shock Absorber (vodka, rum, triple sec, melon sour mix and Seven Up), plus non-alcholic drinks like "The Designated Driver" (pineapple juice, ginger ale and grenadine). Fun for Harley fans of all generations. $$ 🍷🍷

★★½ **JEAN LAFITTE**—68 West 58th Street (near Avenue of the Americas)—751-2323—This bistro has the comfortable feel of a sports jacket with suede elbow patches. It has a dark wood interior peppered with old French movie posters, comfortable banquettes and an easy-going menu that is also a bit retro in feel. Service is most affable. We particularly like to stop in for the $22.50 prix fixe lunch. Onion soup, grilled calamari, salad Jean Lafitte, crab cakes, meat ravioli au gratin, steak tartare, paillard of chicken, chocolate cake, white chocolate mousse, crêpes suzette. $$$½ 🍷🍷

★★★½ **JUDSON GRILL**—152 West 52nd Street (between Seventh and Sixth Avenues)—582-5252—Talented young chef John Villa excels at satisfying the eclectic palates that daily fill this soaring, modernistic space. His appealing menu embraces everything from regional American dishes to Pacific Rim and Moroccan specialties. Manager Chris Cannon assures efficient service, and has also enlivened the wine list with auction finds and hard-to-come-by selections. Indian-spiced salmon tartare, house-smoked Long Island duck breast, peppered tuna loin with braised leeks and green lentils, roasted organic chicken with Moroccan eggplant and cous cous, black Angus steak with sweet potato fries, black plum Napoleon, Judson chocolate sampler. $32.96 pre-theater dinner. $$$½ 🍷🍷🍷🍷

★★★★½ **LA CARAVELLE**—33 West 55th Street (near Avenue of the Americas)—586-4252—Founded in 1960 by protegés of the legendary Henri Soulé, the restaurant has flourished over the past decade under present owners Rita and Andre Jammet, who have forged an effective marriage of traditional and contemporary French cuisine. The beautifully restored Jean Pagès murals and a warm interior studded with peach banquettes recall a leisurely and bygone era. The Jammet's amiable service staff maintains impeccable standards. Chef Cyril Renaud (formerly sous-chef at Bouley) has lightened up La Caravelle's menu with creativity and flair. Snails wrapped in cabbage leaves, quenelles of pike with sauce Nantua, sautéed foie gras with baked apple cake, roasted tuna with coriander and rosemary-flavored compote, sesame-breaded guinea hen in carrot juice with wild mushrooms, venison filet with poivrade sauce, warm banana tart, peanut crunch with white chocolate mousse, fondant au chocolat. Fixed price dinner $62. $$$$$ 🍷🍷🍷🍷

★★★★ **LA CÔTE BASQUE**—60 West 55th Street (between Fifth Avenue and Avenue of the Americas)—688-6525—Under the direction of chef/owner Jean-Jacques Rachou, you bask here in a forty-year tradition of fine dining. The new space is very much a reincarnation of the old location—pale yellow walls, Riviera murals, dark beams—but the experience is fresher, more vibrant, yet somehow soothing. The food is deliciously satisfying and the staff more willing to please than ever. Lobster terrine, potatoes stuffed with snails, tartare of cured and smoked salmon, fresh Dover sole, roasted cod with truffled leeks, spring lamb stew with citrus confit, cassoulet du chef Jean-Jacques au confit du canard, wood-broiled chicken breast with lemon risotto. Razor-thin crusted apple tart, tortini di cappuccino, black peppermint bombe. Fixed price lunch is a steal at $33. $$$$$ 🍷🍷🍷🍷

★★★★★ **LE BERNARDIN**—155 West 51st Street (between 7th Avenue and Avenue of the Americas)—489-1515—This is an imposing and grand space with classic maritime paintings that creates an ideal backdrop for sparkling seafood. The overall mood is supremely elegant, but serious. The staff is professional in its every move and the wine list one of the finest in the city. The pre-eminence of Le Bernardin remains a testament to the dedication of Maguy Lecoze and the memory of her brother Gilbert, whose death in 1994 robbed American gastronomy of one of its great talents. Maguy has forged ahead with veteran chef Eric Ripert, whose own superb style is evident in Le Bernardin's refined cuisine. Mint- and cumin-spiked tuna tartare, scallops with truffle oil, fricassée of mussels, clams and oysters, truffled lobster and celeriac "cappuccino," paupiette of black bass and cabbage with foie gras and truffles, halibut in a marinière of cockles, potatoes and leeks. Florian Bellanger is proving himself a superior pastry chef with lime millefeuille, pear fantasy, black currant clafoutis. Fixed price lunch $42. Fixed price dinner $68. 🍷🍷🍷🍷🍷

★★★ **LEDA**—871 Seventh Avenue (between 55th and

56th Streets)—582-7500—Designer Morris Nathanson has created a grand (180-seat) but romantic setting with hand-painted mosaics, antique Mediterranean fabrics, Greek amphoras and an abundance of gold leaf. Chef David McKenty brings Mediterranean cooking into modern focus, relying on indigenous ingredients and his own command of western cooking techniques. Mixed bean and autumn squash soup with herbed ricotta, grilled Portuguese sardines, grilled marinated octopus, lobster lasagna with spinach leaves, thyme-roasted Chilean sea bass with a stew of white beans and chorizo, cornmeal-crusted monkfish, chocolate semi-freddo. Fixed price lunch $19.97. Pre-theater dinner $29.95. $$$$ 🍷🍷🍷🍷

★★★★★ **LES CÉLÉBRITÉS**—153 West 58th Street (near Avenue of the Americas in the Essex House)—247-0300—This bright jewel-like dining room is a haven within the Essex House hotel. Its diverting and quirky artwork is painted by celebrities; hence the name. More important, it has become a showcase for chef Christian Delouvrier's stellar cuisine, which has risen to the top of NYC's roster. Delouvrier's food is neither trendy nor derivative. It is solidly grounded in French tradition. Paupiettes of smoked and fresh tuna, leek and potato soup with sautéed Scottish langoustines, "burger" of foie gras with tangy Granny Smith apples, grilled halibut with asparagus and morels, open lasagna with grilled loin and leg of rabbit, roasted guinea fowl with fettuccine and white truffles. The cheese service is a terrific array of beautifully ripe selections, and for dessert, sorbets and soft-centered chocolate torte. $$$$$ 🍷🍷🍷🍷🍷

★★★½ **LIMONCELLO**—777 Seventh Avenue at 51st Street (in the Michelangelo Hotel)—582-7932—Romeo De Gobbi, former proprietor of Le Pactole and a 14-year veteran of Le Cirque, has returned to his Italian roots with this charming new trattoria. The interior is simple yet cheery, with earthen hues and contemporary murals. Downstairs, there's a popular cigar bar called the Grotto Club. Tortino of polenta with shrimp and fontina cheese in a porcini sauce, mussels and Manila clam soup, spaghetti al limoncello served with garlic, hot red pepper and lemon zest, grilled filet of salmon, confit and breast of duckling, poussin with mascarpone polenta, fresh fruit tarts, sorbets. $$$$ 🍷🍷🍷

★★½ **MANGIA E BEVI**—800 Ninth Avenue (corner 53rd Street)—956-3976—A highly spirited, retro-looking Italian restaurant with a pleasing menu and remarkably low prices. Good pizzas, and appetizing pastas, including pappardelle delisioso, priced under $10. The most expensive entree, grilled bistecca, is only $13.50. Don't be surprised when the proprietor and waiters break into song and pass out tambourines to customers mid way through dinner; it's all part of the eat, drink and be merry show. Reservations are problematic, so expect a wait. $$ 🍷🍷

★★★★ **MANHATTAN OCEAN CLUB**—57 West 58th Street (near Avenue of the Americas)—371-7777—A sleek and stylish interior adorned with Picasso ceramics and distinctive green-and-white checkered linens makes this two-tiered restaurant one of the most attractive spots for seafood dining, ideal for a business lunch. Talented chef Jonathan Parker prepares wonderful daily specials while maintaining traditional favorites. Seared tuna and salsa verde, baked oysters with morel cream, superb Ocean Club crab cakes, grilled sea scallops with marinated seaweed, rosemary-crusted red snapper, swordfish au poivre, plus standbys like grilled catch of the day, chocolate "bag", crème brûlée, fruit Napoleon. $$$$½ 🍷🍷🍷🍷

★★★ **MICHAEL'S**—24 West 55th Street (between Fifth and Sixth Avenues)—767-0555—At lunchtime, the dining rooms are packed with dark suits drinking Coca Cola, iced tea or Pellegrino (a pity, considering the wine list is so interesting), all seemingly digging into a grilled chicken breast and enormous mounds of salad. This is California cuisine à la Michael McCarty, the progenitor of the form, who has established a midtown mecca for the business lunch (dinner is a bit more subdued). An eclectic art collection provides the backdrop for a regional menu (which lists the provenance of practically every ingredient). Service can be frenzied. Cilantro broth with Montauk calamari, Hackensack bresaola with arugula an parmesan, risotto with Maine lobster, clams, mussels and scallops, Canadian salmon with tomato vinaigrette, grilled Chicago sweetbreads with Spanish capers, duck with Grand Marnier and California oranges, tarte tatin, walnut torte "Heath bar," chocolate raspberry mousse cake. $$$$$ 🍷🍷🍷🍷

★★½ **MICKEY MANTLE'S**—42 Central Park South

(near Sixth Avenue)—688-7777—You can practically conjure up the whole scenario before even setting foot in this fun mid-town eatery. Oversized television screens throughout tuned to—what else—baseball games past and present. Lots of ball club paraphernalia—bats, gloves, uniforms, etc. The food is hearty and portions—be they burgers, fries, or salads—are very large. A great homage to a great ball-player, and fun for kids, little and large. $$$½ 🍷🍷

★★★ **THE OAK ROOM AND BAR**—768 Fifth Avenue (at 59th Street in the Plaza Hotel)—546-5330—The majesty of this legendary, utterly romantic dining room with its oak columns and soft lighting is unique in America, a reminder of what grand dining was once all about. Now, after decades of mediocre food, the kitchen has sublimated the basic steaks, chops and seafood menu to a standard we'd encourage others to match, although we wish prices were lower for this sort of menu. Service is gracious and attentive; even the pianist shows a remarkable talent for discreet entertainment. The Oak Room Bar is as lively as ever. Crabmeat Imperial, chateaubriand for two, swordfish with fresh shrimp, chocolate mousse cake. $$$$$ 🍷🍷

★★ **O'NEAL'S**—49 West 64th Street (between Broadway and Central Park West)—787-4663—Convenient to Lincoln Center, crowds flock here for simple fare served up in casual surroundings. There's onion soup, mushroom pie, chicken pot pie, and a broad variety of salads priced under $13. Sandwiches are priced under $9.00 and include smoked salmon, grilled chicken, roasted eggplant and roast beef on sourdough. $$ 🍷🍷

★★★★ **OSTERIA DEL CIRCO**—120 West 55th Street (near Avenue of the Americas)—265-3636—A $3-million design concept by Adam Tihany with circus-inspired monkey mobiles, striped tenting, bright banners and a trapeze above the mahogany bar sets the stage for Mario, Marco and Mauro Maccioni's fanciful trattoria. Not surprisingly, these affable scions of fabled Manhattan restaurateur Sirio Maccioni (Le Cirque 2000, q.v.) attract a spate of Le Cirque regulars, along with a predictable quotient of celebs, making this a very hot ticket. But the secret attraction here is their mother Egi, whose many recipes are executed by a talented kitchen team. Soup with thirty vegetables,

Egi's ravioli with spinach, ricotta butter and sage, pizza "Circo", with tomato, mascarpone and prosciutto, grilled yellowfin tuna, monkfish with mussels and peas, roast pork loin arista, frozen tiramisù, bomboloni. $$$½ 🍷🍷🍷

★★★ **PATSY'S**—236 West 56th Street (near Broadway)—247-3491—A bastion of Southern Italian cooking, Patsy's is a good example of consistency and dedication. The decor has been lightened in recent years, but the celebrity photos still form a gallery of stars—Frank Sinatra, Paul Simon, Liza Minnelli, Charleton Heston and others—who really do eat here and even protested publicly when a local food critic lambasted the place in print. You'll certainly not leave hungry and you'll find the gutsy pastas and entrées to your liking, from the wonderful antipasto of sausage, mozzarella and eggplant to the baked rigatoni sorrentino to the garlicky chicken scarpariello. A good spot before the theater or afterwards, and ideal for a quiet midtown lunch. Fixed price $19.50 lunch; $28.50 pre-theater dinner. $$$½ 🍷🍷

★★★ **PETROSSIAN**—182 West 58th Street (at Seventh Avenue)—245-2214—This dark, cool, deco-style space has the feel of an exotic club that has seen more festive times. Indifferent blue-blazered captains compound the effect. "Membership"—in the form of the lavish $135 "Les Années Folles" special, which proffers beluga and sevruga caviar plus foie gras and sturgeon—is pricey. Go for the less expensive "teasers" of smoked river trout with egg crêpe and horseradish sauce, or smoked cod roe on cheese crisps. Alternatively, there's roast duck with lentils, loin of Arctic venison with wild mushrooms, lemon tart with lemon custard and caramel, Valrhona chocolate soufflé with maple ice cream, vanilla crème brûlée. Pre-theater dinner at $35. $$$$$ 🍷🍷🍷

★★★★½ **PICHOLINE**—35 West 64th Street (between Columbus and Central Park West)—724-8585—The interior has a rich and elegant glow—terra-cotta silk walls, tapestries, plushly-upholstered cane-back chairs and banquettes, plus signature "Picholine" plates. There's a very handsome private "wine cellar" room that seats eight. Chef-owner Terrance Brennan is the ultimate perfectionist. His Mediterranean-inspired menu is a constantly evolving masterpiece, rich in textures and nuances of flavor. The wild mushroom and duck risotto is a must try, an ideal meal-in-one before a performance at nearby Lincoln Center. Fricassee of Pemaquid oysters, lentil salad with duck prosciutto, carpaccio of tuna, spiced and barbecued quail, black bass tartare with osetra caviar, Moroccan spiced loin of lamb, warm apple-cranberry empanadas, hazelnut crunch semifreddo, "pear-pear-pear." Leave room for the spectacular cheese selection. $$$$ 🍷🍷🍷

★½ **PLANET HOLLYWOOD**—140 West 57th Street (between Avenue of the Americas and Seventh Avenue)—333-7827—With such celebrated co-owners as Arnold, Sylvester, Bruce and Demi, Planet Hollywood has generated more than its fare share of publicity. Not surprisingly, the place is festooned with props, posters, and photos from famous flicks. Planet Hollywood draws an eclectic crowd ranging from teens and families to the simply curious, all of whom wait in line for a table, hoping to catch a glimpse of a visiting celeb. The menu, however, is hardly a hit. Lots of junk food like nachos, Italachos (deep-fried pizza dough with barbecue sauce, guacamole and sour cream), burgers and sandwiches, with a smattering of grown-up fare like grilled swordfish, and chicken. $$ 🍷

★★½ **REDEYE GRILL**—890 Seventh Avenue (at 56th Street)—541-9000—This vast space with a front room overlooking Carnegie Hall is the latest addition to Shelley Fireman's growing empire (Trattoria del Arte, Brooklyn Diner, Hosteria Fiorella, etc.) The operative words here are shrimp and fun; Redeye, with over a dozen different shrimp preparations on the menu, is also home to the "dancing shrimp"—curvaceous swiveling shrimp sculptures which preside over a glistening raw bar. The main room, with its festive murals, offers something for diners of all ages: Chinese, Mexican and California dishes vie with smoked fish and sashimi. Don't miss the dancing shrimp Louie for its presentation alone, but skip the lobster cobb royale, which is overpriced at $28.75. For landlubbers there's a generous cheeseburger, steak frites and Baja chicken with chorizo sausage. Banana cream pie, chocolate truffle cake, strawberry cheesecake are all quite satisfying. $$$ 🍷🍷🍷

★★★★ **REMI**—145 West 53rd Street (near Seventh Avenue)—581-4242—Under his own roof, the fabled architect Adam Tihany has created a lively dining room with a towering Venetian mural that arches from the ceiling, with smartly-striped blue and white banquettes and striped parquet floors that continue the motif. The cordial staff are also clad in stripes. Talented chef/co-owner Francesco Antonucci has crafted a menu to match, highly compelling in presentation and flavor. Remi is a great spot for a midtown business lunch or a pre-theater meal. Shrimp cakes, mushroom stew with truffled soft-polenta, seared sea scallops with white beans, penne with crisped zucchini, cannelloni stuffed with veal, grilled salmon with green cabbage, frozen chocolate hazelnut and amaretto zabaglione, apple and mascarpone cheesecake. To cap off a leisurely dinner, there's a good selection of grappa and Ports. Alfresco dining in summer. $$$½ 🍷🍷🍷

★★★★ **RESTAURANT RAPHAEL**—33 West 54th Street (between Fifth and Sixth Avenues)—582-8993—This understated space with muted Provençal tones imparts a cozy townhouse feeling. The dedication of owners Raphael and Myra Edery combined with the artful skills of chef David McInerney make a successful mix. You can expect jewel-like presentations, with food and plate coordinated in perfect harmony. The wine list is interesting, but avoid ordering pricey house wines by the glass. Proximity to MoMA makes this an ideal luncheon destination. Fricassee of chanterelles in red wine reduction sauce, goat cheese and roasted pepper terrine, herb-roasted oysters with ragoût of wild mushrooms, grilled tuna medallions with potato, leek and mushroom gratin, pan-roasted wild striped bass with braised escarole, duck confit with white beans, beef tartar with white truffle toast crisps, frozen honey parfait, tarte tatin, warm flourless chocolate cake. $$$$$ 🍷🍷🍷

★★★ **RUTH'S CHRIS STEAK HOUSE**—148 West 51st Street (near Seventh Avenue)—245-9600—Another link in the now-vast chain out of New Orleans, Ruth's Chris (owned by Ruth Fertel) is a big hit for its Broadway location, and generous portions. The meat is good, cooked at extreme high heat, but the side orders could be better. For dessert there's key lime pie and pecan pie. The wine list is first rate. $$$$½ 🍷🍷🍷

★★★★½ **SAN DOMENICO**—240 Central Park South (off Columbus Circle)—265-5959—This is a handsome dining room with warm woods, floral displays, classic artwork and very comfortable seating, presided over by the discerning Tony May and his genial daughter Marisa. San Domenico remains one of the most consistently gratifying destinations in the city. New chef Odette Fada has put her own sophisticated stamp on the menu while retaining signature dishes such as uovo in ravioli with truffle butter, jumbo shrimp with cannellini beans, homemade spaghetti with tomato and basil. Fada's seasonal specials include risotto with parmesan and white truffles, beef tartare with marinated mushrooms, roasted baby goat with broccoli rabe and polenta, braised rabbit marinated in red wine. For dessert, there's tiramisù San Domenico, semifreddo with passion fruit in mango sauce, hazelnut souffle in white chocolate sauce. Spectacular wine list. Fixed price pre-theater dinner at $29.50. $$$$$ 🍷🍷🍷🍷

★★½ **SETTE MoMA**—11 West 53rd Street (by day enter via The Museum of Modern Art; after 5 PM, enter at 12 West 54th Street)—708-9710—This 200-seat trattoria overlooking the museum's sculpture court has become a destination, due to saavy Nino Esposito and Genaro Virtucci, who own Sette Mezzo, Vico Madison (q.v.). They have met the challenge of providing satisfying fare within the confines of a bustling institution. Service has improved and the menu is more manageable. Endive and frisée salad with gorgonzola, warm goat cheese wrapped in eggplant with yellow pepper coulis, spaghetti alla chitarra, veal ravioli in a wild mushroom sauce. At lunch, diners must pay the museum's general admission of $7.50. No evening entrance fees. Closed Wednesday. $$$½ 🍷🍷🍷

★★★ **SHUN LEE DYNASTY**—43 West 65th Street (off Broadway)—595-8895—Black banquettes and dragon lanterns set the stage for some creative dining. Owner Michael Tong's menu is certainly innovative but some standbys like giant prawns in black bean sauce, and sole on its crispy bone fail to deliver. Steamed dumplings, Szechuan wonton, Szechuan pork. The Shun Lee Café (sort of a restaurant within a restaurant) features dim sum as well as "street food," such as suckling pig and beef congee. The café is less interesting in comparison to its parent. $$$ 🍷🍷🍷

★★ **SOUP KITCHEN INTERNATIONAL**—259 West 55th Street (near Eighth Avenue)—757-7730—This is it: The famous—some would say notorious—soup kitchen whose owner, Al Yeganeh, was parodied as the mean-spirited "Soup Nazi" on "Seinfeld" last year. Despite Yeganeh's protest of the sobriquet, the fellow doesn't suffer indecisive patrons gladly. So get in line, know what you want and move along. The soups change daily, but you can count on a broad variety, ranging from shrimp bisque to chicken brocolli to veal goulash. Is it worth it? Yeah, yeah, yeah—keep moving! $

★★★½ **TAPIKA**—950 Eighth Avenue (at 56th Street)—397-3737—The talented David Walzog, former chef of Arizona 206, presides over this Southwestern range which was formerly the Symphony Café. Now far less sedate in atmosphere, the place has been fearlessly transformed by designer David Rockwell. A cowboy motif predominates, with branding irons emblazoned on the walls and a glowing terra cotta interior. Walzog's menu is robust and zesty. Spicy black bean purée with ground chorizo, tequila-cured salmon, barbecued short ribs, roasted red snapper with pickled shallots, coriander-crusted tuna, bacon-wrapped organic turkey with whole wheat stuffing and toasted chile sauce, chile-rubbed salmon. Banana chocolate parfait with hazelnut praline, southwestern profiteroles. Pre-theater dinner $31. $$$$ 🍷🍷🍷

★★½ **TRATTORIA DELL'ARTE**—900 Seventh Avenue (between 56th and 57th Streets)—245-9800—This is a convenient place to repair to before or after a Carnegie Hall performance—so long as you ignore the oversized wall hangings of unsightly ears, noses, etc. The trattoria menu has evolved and improved, and service is bustling. Antipasto platter, spicy chicken sausages with red peppers, hot foccacia sandwiches, razor-thin pizza prosciutto, risotto with asparagus, cannoli, tiramisù. $$$ 🍷🍷

★★ **WEST 63rd STREET STEAKHOUSE**—44 West 63rd Street (near Columbus Avenue)—246-6363—A glowy, showy, paneled room with a dotted leopard carpet and amoeba-like dotted paintings. Combine this with piped-in music, and you feel as if you were eating in a hotel dining room somewhere out of state. (In fact, this restaurant is indeed located on the second floor of the Empire Radisson Hotel, opposite Lincoln Center.) Caesar salad, crab cakes, above-average fried zucchini, rack of lamb, filet mignon, New York cheesecake, strawberry shortcake. $$$$$ 🍷🍷🍷

SIXTY-SIXTH STREET TO NINETY-SIXTH STREET (EAST)

★★½ **7TH REGIMENT MESS**—643 Park Avenue (at 66th Street)—744-4107—Set in the 7th Regiment Armory, this enchanting restaurant is an antique dream, with massive dark wood, a terrific old oak bar, and some of the finest down-to-earth American fare you'll find anywhere—simple roast beef, chicken, turkey, mashed potatoes, and everything that goes with them. $$½

★★ **BARAONDA**—1429 Second Avenue (at 75th Street)—288-8555—Extremely quiet by day, by night, this attractive trattoria transforms itself into a highly animated and bristling single's spot to sample simple pastas (the sliced sautéed artichokes are also worth a try) and above all, to savor the crowd scene. Grilled eggplant, shrimp risotto, taglioni with tomato and basil, ricotta cheesecake. $$½ 🍷🍷

★★★ **BELLA BLU**—967 Lexington Avenue (between 70th and 71st Streets)—988-4624—There is great whimsy in this Gaudi-esque remake of the former Yuppie haven Shelby's. With its vivid, undulating murals and "devil-may-care" ceiling motif, this place has great humor—and more importantly, flavor. Deftly managed by Attilio Fragna and presided over by chef Marc Vetri, the menu combines both sophistication and appealing simplicity. Depending on your appetite, you may want to start—and stop—with one of 18 tempting pizzas, like the Lexington (spicy sausage, tomato, mozzarella and mushrooms), from the wood-burning oven. Alternatively, consider sautéed baby artichokes with pistachio and parmesan, crabmeat croquettes with sautéed leeks, spaghettini with roasted lobster, pounded and breaded chicken breast with potato purée, sliced dry Angus beef over arugula, pistachio crème brûlée, chocolate terrine. Amex only. $$$ 🍷🍷🍷

★★½ **BISTRO DU NORD**—1312 Madison Avenue (corner of 93rd Street)—289-0997—This is a very tiny, very French bistro with paper-topped tables and fabulous vintage-Avedon photographs covering the walls. It's a

SIXTY-SIXTH TO NINETY-SIXTH STREET (EAST)

1 7th Regiment Mess
2 Mediterraneo
3 L'Ardoise
4 L'Absinthe
5 The Right Bank
6 The Polo
7 Lumi
8 Café Evergreen
9 Bella Blu
10 Sette Mezzo
11 Le Petit Hulot
12 The Kiosk
13 Syrah
14 Petaluma
15 Letizia
16 Café Crocodile
17 EJ's Luncheonette
18 Lenox Room
19 Willow
20 Vivolo
21 J.G. Melon
22 Mezzaluna
23 Coco Pazzo
24 Mortimer's
25 Quisisana
26 Orienta
27 Baraonda
28 Portico
29 Voulez Vous
30 Il Monello
31 Jim McMullen
32 Daniel
33 The Three Guys
34 Lusardi's
35 Savann Est
36 Sant Ambroeus
37 Sofia
38 Trois Jean
39 Parma
40 Quatorze Bis
41 Sistina
42 Tiramisu
43 Lobster Club
44 Parioli Romanissimo
45 Butterfield 81
46 Mazzei
47 Etats Unis
48 Le Réfuge
49 Zocalo
50 Girasole
51 Erminia
52 King's Carriage House
53 Primavera
54 Elio's
55 Paola's Restaurant
56 Cha Yen
57 Demarchelier
58 Elaine's
59 Sarabeth's Kitchen
60 Table d'Hôte
61 Vico Madison
62 Bistro du Nord
63 Demi

CENTR
PARK

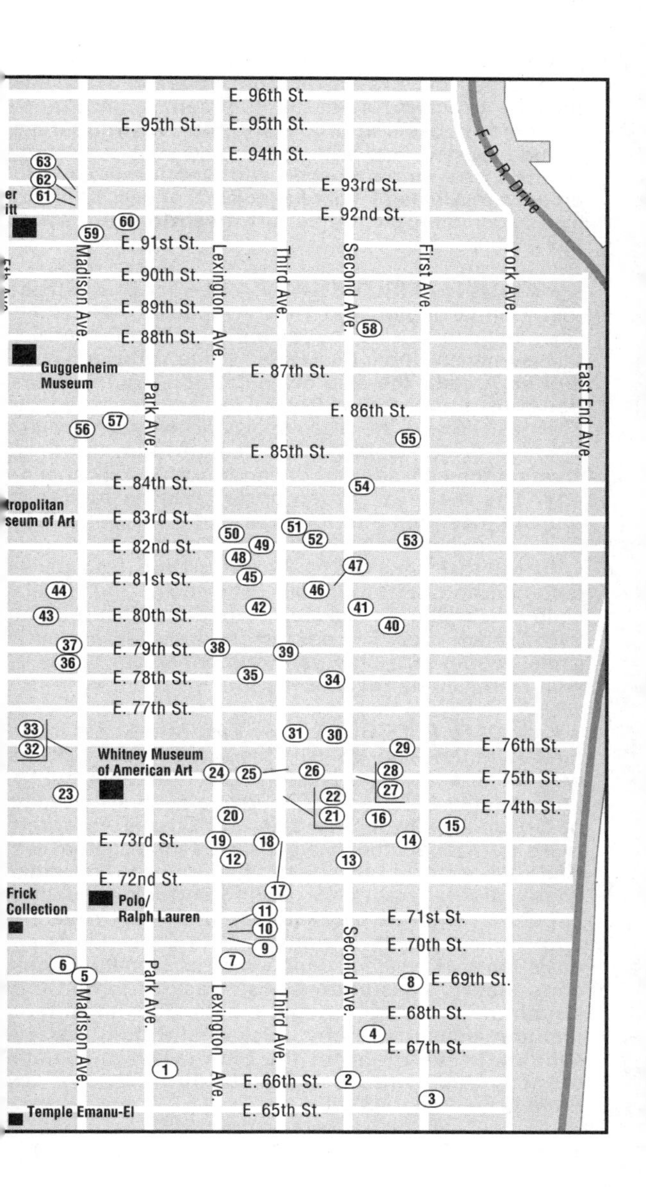

E. 96th St.
E. 95th St.
E. 95th St.
E. 94th St.
E. 93rd St.
E. 92nd St.
F. D. R. Drive
63
62
61
60
59
E. 91st St.
E. 90th St.
E. 89th St.
E. 88th St.
Madison Ave.
Lexington Ave.
Third Ave.
Second Ave.
First Ave.
York Ave.
58
Guggenheim Museum
E. 87th St.
Park Ave.
E. 86th St.
East End Ave.
57
56
55
E. 85th St.
E. 84th St.
54
Museum of Art
E. 83rd St.
51
50
52
53
E. 82nd St.
49
48
47
E. 81st St.
45
46
44
43
42
41
E. 80th St.
40
37
36
E. 79th St.
38
39
E. 78th St.
35
34
E. 77th St.
33
32
31
30
29
E. 76th St.
Whitney Museum of American Art
24
25
26
28
27
E. 75th St.
23
22
21
E. 74th St.
20
16
15
E. 73rd St.
19
18
14
12
13
E. 72nd St.
17
Frick Collection
Polo/ Ralph Lauren
11
10
9
E. 71st St.
E. 70th St.
Second Ave.
7
6
5
8
E. 69th St.
Madison Ave.
Park Ave.
Lexington Ave.
Third Ave.
E. 68th St.
4
E. 67th St.
1
E. 66th St.
2
3
Temple Emanu-El
E. 65th St.

bright and blithe Carnegie Hill destination. We definitely prefer the downstairs room, where you can dine heartily on chef Xavier Duclos' saucisson chaud, steamed mussels and country paté. Main courses include roasted duck with apples and calvados sauce, roasted free-range chicken with shallot sauce and breaded rack of lamb with flageolets. For dessert, flourless chocolate cake, apple tart, fresh fruit in phyllo. $$$½ 🍷🍷

★★★ **BUTTERFIELD 81**—168-170 East 81st Street (between Lexington and Third Avenues)—288-2700—Once the site of a sleepy restaurant called Pinocchio, this is now an Upper East Side "scene" presided over by Ken Aretsky (he also owns Patroon, q.v.) with his daughter and co-chef Beth Aretsky. Designed by Thomas O'Brien, the place sports richly-glazed walls, wooden floors, dark banquettes and dim lighting, creating the sensation of dining in a chic milk chocolate. The menu is contemporary, with a focus on preparations from the wood-burning oven. Butterfield 81 Caesar salad, marinated tuna tartare with ginger, wild mushroom risotto, wood-grilled foie gras, caramelized pork tenderloin with ancho and pasilla chile rub, grilled rib eye steak, wood-fired hamburger with French fries. For dessert there's even a wood-grilled apple tart, plus Valrhona chocolate brownie with crème anglaise. $$$$ 🍷🍷🍷

★★★★ **CAFÉ CROCODILE**—354 East 74th Street (near First Avenue)—249-6619—This town house setting with a country feeling is adorned with murals, subtly printed tablecloths, and of course, a copious quantity of crocodiles. Owners Andrée and Charlie Abramoff make their diners feel like guests. Every dish conveys Andrée's personal touch, and Charlie's passion for his wine cellar is exemplary. Don't overlook appealing appetizers such as pissaladiere, "three duck plate," and smoked haddock mousse. Café Crocodile is an oasis for cold weather dining with its signature cous cous, hearty cassoulet, classic rack of lamb, and boudin noir au chou rouge. Lighter Provençal fare includes seasoned baby chicken and pan-roasted salmon. Leave room for the bittersweet chocolate crunch, and wild cherries clafoutis. $$$½ 🍷🍷🍷
Fixed price dinner $33.50.

★★★ **CAFÉ EVERGREEN**—1288 First Avenue (at 69th

Street)—744-3266—A bustling open kitchen is scene to an enticing Hong Kong style Cantonese menu with a wide array of innovative appetizers, delicious dim sum, and noodles. The look is simple and uncontrived, and so is the well priced fare. Cilantro shrimp dumplings, fluffy half moon dumplings, pork dumplings, prawns with X.O. and chili sauce, crispy orange beef, General Tso's spicy crispy pan-fried noodles, roasted pork chow fun. No MSG is added. Over a dozen well-chosen wines by the glass. $$ 🍷🍷🍷🍷

★★½ **CHA YEN**—1165 Madison Avenue (between 85th and 86th Streets)—737-8772—Owner Patrick Demarchelier (Jean Lafite, Demarchelier) has engaged chef Phai Rot, a Bangkok native, to preside over this pleasant, no-frills neighborhood place. Its blonde woods, complemented by a black-and-white linoleum floor, create an almost sauna-like feeling. "Basket weaving 101" chairs, paper lanterns and ceiling fans complete the Thai look. The menus is satisfying and authentic, with very fresh ingredients and a good balance of lightly-spiced flavors and textures. Thai spring rolls, Thai dumplings, shrimp fried noodles, sweet and sour chicken, beef massaman, green curry shrimps, banana roll. Fixed price lunch $12.50. $$$ 🍷🍷

★★★ **COCO PAZZO**—23 East 74th Street (off Madison Avenue)—794-0205—A popular and casually chic Upper East side trattoria with pale yellow walls and a handsome bar up front. The staff is attentive, and new chef Maurizio Marfoglia delivers a satisfying Tuscan menu. Grilled portabello mushroom caps, seared tuna rolled in black pepper, garganelli with prosciutto and radicchio, pappardelle with rabbit ragu, bistecca Fiorentina, poached halibut, semifreddo, tartuffo. $$$$ 🍷🍷🍷

★★★★★ **DANIEL**—20 East 76th Street (near Madison Avenue)—288-0033—With its wonderful glow, neutral tones, plush upholstery and sensational flowers, restaurant Daniel is one of the most enchanting and captivating spots in town. Chef/owner Daniel Boulud is one of America's greatest culinary talents and his ever-changing French menu incorporates the very freshest ingredients. The staff is knowledgeable, professional and always willing to please. The wine list is extensive but not necessarily expensive. First-timers should consider signature dishes like curried tuna tartare with radishes, or sea scallops layered with black truffles.

The seasonal menus are superb, starting with soups like curried cauliflower with lobster and coriander. Indulge in sautéed foie gras with blood oranges, casserole of porcini mushrooms and sweetbreads, roasted saddle of rabbit with olives, roasted Pacific salmon with horseradish and white beans, roasted rib of beef with marrow and chanterelles. Pastry chef François Payard's splendid desserts include apple sorbet in apple syrup with dried apple chips, chilled pistachio cake, bittersweet chocolate bombe with crème brûlée. $$$$$ 🍷🍷🍷🍷

★★½ **DEMARCHELIER**—50 East 86th Street (between Madison and Park Avenues)—249-6300—Veteran restaurateur Patrick Demarchelier (Jean Lafitte, Cha Yen, q.v.) has devised a winning formula for a popular neighborhood destination—warm yellow walls, comfy banquettes, grape-motif lace curtains, ceiling fans and a carved wooden bar with regulars occupying every stool. The bistro food is simple and honest—onion soup, warm goat cheese salad, salad Niçoise, mussels marinière, grilled salmon, steak tartare, veal paillard, crème caramel, tarte tatin, chocolate mousse cake. $$$ 🍷🍷

★★½ **DEMI**—1316 Madison Avenue (at 93rd Street)—534-3475—This charming Carnegie Hill townhouse sports soothing pink walls, fresh roses on the tables and an air of intimacy. It is an ideal spot to repair to after visiting nearby neighborhood museums. Chef Terrance John offers the likes of chilled Champagne and melon soup, country salad with warm goat cheese and polenta croutons, lobster ravioli with chopped tomatoes, grilled shrimp with asparagus and fresh thyme risotto, red chili crusted salmon with braised spinach, hazelnut praline cheesecake, wild berry sorbet. $$$ 🍷🍷🍷

★★ **EJ'S LUNCHEONETTE**—1271 Third Avenue (at 73rd Street)—472-0600—A popular East Side spot (with a West Side sibling, q.v.) for a reasonably priced family breakfast, brunch, lunch or dinner. The interior decor is somewhat more contrived than the crosstown branch, but the menu is just as well executed. A wide array of breakfast dishes includes flapjacks, waffles, and eggs galore. Lunch or dinner consists of a broad selection of sandwiches, burgers and salads, some designed for the health conscious. You can order a traditional turkey club sandwich or opt for the EJ version, made with avocado and chicken. Don't overlook the addictive French fries, milk shakes and malteds. No reservations. No credit cards. $$ 🍷

○ **ELAINE'S**—1703 Second Avenue (near 88th Street)—534-8103—A truly awful great place. It may still reign supreme as a literary/celebrity hang-out for the likes of Woody Allen, Gay Talese, and David Halberstam, and owner Elaine Kauffman makes her chums feel coddled. But the food is nowhere near as stellar as the clientele, and the waiters think they're doing you a favor by serving you. $$$½ 🍷

★★★ **ELIO'S**—1621 Second Avenue (at 84th Street)—772-2242—Festive, though noisy Upper East Side hangout patronized by its fair share of celebs. In fact, the place is so popular that you should factor in a wait for your table as a matter of course. Very dependable pasta preparations, good calamari and veal chops, cheesecake, lemon tart. Good selection of wines. Dinner only. No reservations. $$$½ 🍷🍷

★★½ **ERMINIA**—250 East 83rd Street (between Second and Third Avenues)—879-4284—This remains a warm, romantic and flower-festooned spot with brick walls, lanterns, handkerchief-draped fixtures and candlelight. The traditional menu is also a bit of a throwback. Tossed green salad, mozzarella with roasted peppers, carpaccio of salmon, veal chop, striped bass with clams, rolled pasta, cheese cake, tartuffo strawberries with cold zabaglione. Service is efficient but can be a tad haughty. $$$$$ 🍷🍷

★★★½ **ETATS UNIS**—241 East 81st Street (near Second Avenue)—517-8826—It is amazing how this diminutive restaurant with an even more minuscule kitchen consistently produces grand results. Presided over by the Rapp family, Etats Unis is casual and inviting, with an appealing interior full of architectural whimsy (and sidewalk dining in season). It's a comforting spot to sample an ever-changing menu, including mussel bisque, peaches with prosciutto and basil, roasted pepper salad with grilled squid and onions, charcoal-grilled wild striped bass with roasted tomato, oven-roasted free-range chicken with bacon and sage, seared scallops with roasted pears, chocolate soufflé, ginger chocolate torte with whipped cream, angel food cake with red wine sauce. $$$½ 🍷🍷

★★½ **GIRASOLE**—151 East 82nd Street (between Lexington and Third Avenues)—772-6690—A neighborhood standby with a pleasing pastel interior that can rack up the decibels when crowded to capacity. The kitchen's output more than compensates. Polenta with gorgonzola, spiedino with smoked mozzarella, sautéed baby artichoke, grilled organic Cornish hen with peppercorns, veal chop with capers and tapenade, gelati, ricotta cheesecake. $$$½ 🍷🍷

★★★★ **IL MONELLO**—1460 Second Avenue (near 76th Street)—535-9310—Il Monello remains a highly popular, upscale neighborhood trattoria under the ownership of the indefatigable Adi Giovanetti (also proprietor of Il Nido, q.v.). It replicates some of the flagship's trademark touches, such as tableside preparation of certain dishes. Service is highly efficient and energetic. Calamari with baby greens and balsamic vinaigrette, Caesar salad, buffalo carpaccio with truffle oil, ravioli with organic greens and mascarpone, red snapper in a pine nut crust, sautéed rack of lamb in a sage and butter sauce, breaded veal chop with tomato basil and onion salad, cheesecake, Grand Marnier semifreddo. $$$$ 🍷🍷🍷🍷

★★ **J.G. MELON**—1291 Third Avenue (at 74th Street)—744-0585—This popular neighborhood pub bristles with activity until the wee hours. The casual decor is enlivened by paintings and prints of—what else—the melon in myriad manifestations. Melon's attracts a diverse uptown crowd. Excellent bacon-cheeseburgers, chile, club sandwiches and cottage fries. Great bar. Good Bloody Marys and Bullshots. No reservations. No credit cards. $$ 🍷

★★ **JIM McMULLEN**—1341 Third Avenue (near 76th Street)—861-4700—Since the late '70s, Jim McMullen has been drawing a crowd of regulars (ladies who lunch by day and a more animated set by night) to this uptown spot for simple food such as roasted chicken, grilled tuna and the like. Now that McMullen himself has resumed command of the operation, the menu has been enlivened, with more ambitious salads and pastas. Of particular interest is the wide variety of wines available by the glass, which rotate on a daily basis. $$½ 🍷🍷🍷

★★½ **KING'S CARRIAGE HOUSE**—251 East 82nd Street (between Second and Third Avenues)—734-5490—Set on two floors of an enchanting townhouse, this is surely a romantic spot, even if the menu does not entirely live up to the setting. Quail and foie gras terrine, salad of roquefort and walnuts, grilled shrimp over field greens and avocado, poussin with morel sauce, filet mignon with stilton sauce and potato dauphin, strawberry rhubarb tart, mocha hazelnut cake. $34 fixed price dinner. $$$$ 🍷🍷

★★½ **THE KIOSK**—1007 Lexington Avenue (between 72nd and 73rd Streets)—535-6000—This small and stylish interior with—what else?—newspaper logos bordering its walls, brings a downtown feeling uptown. Bright metal tabletops illuminate local faces. Service is friendly. Food is safe, easy, and predictable. Gazpacho, spicy grilled calamari with watercress, hamburger, pasta pomodoro, grilled lamb chops with rosemary, chocolate mousse cake. $$$ 🍷🍷

★★★★ **L'ABSINTHE**—227 East 67th Street (near Second Avenue)—794-4950—This may very well be the prettiest bistro in town. It has a flattering glow, comfy banquettes, enormous floral displays, an authentic zinc bar and smartly tiled floors. Chef/partner Jean-Michel Bergougnoux has elevated basic bistro technique to a higher plateau while preserving traditional recipes. Service is precise and unobtrusive. Portions are just the right size and presentation is honest. Mosaic of cèpes and potatoes with pan seared foie gras, fricassee of snails and salsify, shaved parmesan prosciutto chips, saucisson chaud, roasted lobster with fingerling potatoes and mushrooms, slow-braised lean beef, pan-seared loin of lamb with fennel and artichoke vinaigrette, poached chicken in a truffle broth, cheese tray, warm apple tart, warm chocolate cake, pear tart. $$$$½ 🍷🍷🍷

★★★ **LE PETIT HULOT**—973 Lexington Avenue (near 70th Street)—794-9800—Presided over by the amiable Gérard Oliver, Le Petit Hulot serves up pleasing French fare in casual surroundings: white walls, blond woods, bistro chairs, photographs. Upstairs is a smart looking smoking/banquet room. Light salads, pastas, mushroom quiche prevail at lunch. Crab cakes, vegetable terrine, roasted chicken with mashed potatoes, sautéed calf's liver, and roasted cod with tomato and basil garnish the dinner menu. $$$½ 🍷🍷

★★★½ **LE RÉFUGE**—166 East 82nd Street (between Third and Lexington Avenues)—861-4505—A charming Upper East Side haunt, lodged in a comely townhouse, redolent in look and feel of a provincial French bistro. The menu is equally inviting. Crisp vegetable terrine, pea soup, frisée aux lardons, snails in puff pastry, shrimp with cous cous, lobster ravioli, filet of beef salad with endive and arrugula, pommes Normandes. For dessert, try "Vivaldi's Sweet Revenge." (Now with a City Island branch called Le Réfuge Inn.) $17–$23 fixed price pre-theater dinner. $$$ 🍷🍷🍷

★★★½ **THE LENOX ROOM**—1278 Third Avenue (near 73rd Street)—772-0404—With its dramatic floral displays, earth tones and tweedy textures, this lively neighborhood restaurant has evolved into a first-rate destination. It is presided over by the stellar team of Tony Fortuna, one of the best restaurant managers in the city, and top toque Charlie Palmer, chef-owner of Aureole and Alva, plus resident chefs Andy Thompson and Matthew Geraghthy. Diners flock here for the sumptuous raw bar and a contemporary menu with international borrowings. Thai-spiced dumplings, yellowfin tuna tartare, smoked salmon pillow, green lentil and foie gras terrine, risotto of the day, seared salmon with bok choi, roasted loin of lamb with fondant potatoes, lemon custard tart, chocolate pound cake. $$$$ 🍷🍷🍷

★★★ **LETIZIA**—1352 First Avenue (between 72nd and 73rd Streets)—517-2244—A simple neighborhood spot (convenient to Sotheby's) with tile floors, peach walls, and a large collection of photographs. The Sicilian menu is a fascinating amalgam of Italian, Greek, North African and Spanish flavors. Owners Tony and Frank Pecora serve up unusual specials each night. Artichoke hearts stuffed with potato, peas, pine nuts and caciocavallo cheese, breaded and fried rice balls studded with mozzarella, and the classic bucatini sauced with a combination of wild fennel, fresh sardines, raisins and bread crumbs. Not all the specialties are on the printed menu, so ask about them. For dessert, cannolis or candied fruits and chocolate chips. $$$½ 🍷🍷🍷

★★★½ **LOBSTER CLUB**—24 East 80th Street (between Madison and Fifth Avenues)—249-6500—Named after chef/owner Anne Rosensweig's signature dish at Arcadia, her uptown outpost is more casual in style and whimsical in format than the flagship. It's a comfortable, two-story townhouse with brick walls downstairs, and an upper floor dotted with eclectic bric-a-brac. No matter what you order, be sure to sample the crispy rock shrimp with jalapeño tartar sauce. Consider crab and cous cous cakes with tomato remoulade, Moroccan spring rolls, Provençal fries, mom's meatloaf, fish and chips of the day, and of course, the ubiquitous lobster club. For dessert, there's cherry clafoutis, chocolate-and-caramel tart, banana split. The wine list is highly creative. There's also a $24.95 lunch "express"; three courses delivered in under 60 minutes. $$$$ 🍷🍷🍷🍷

★★★ **LUMI**—963 Lexington Avenue (corner 70th Street)—570-2335—This cheery and fresh-looking duplex has fostered debates over the merits of the upstairs and downstairs dining areas. (We prefer the spiffy, cleanly-designed ground floor.) But no matter where you sit, you can expect a satisfying and subtle menu. Antipasti, bresaola with arugula and goat cheese, fried calamari, dumplings filled with artichoke hearts and ricotta, panzotti with pignoli, grilled lamb chops with endive, grilled tuna with cannellini beans, gelati, sorbets, panna cotta. $$$ 🍷🍷

★★½ **LUSARDI'S**—1494 Second Avenue (near 78th Street)—249-2020—A delightful neighborhood trattoria, with a cozy interior and very friendly service, which produces robust Northern Italian fare. Good fried calamari with tomato sauce, grilled smoked mozzarella and radicchio, sun dried tomato ravioli with fontina (in season, why not splurge for an appetizer portion of pasta and white truffles for one of the lowest supplements in town). Sautéed salmon, veal sorpresa, chicken with artichokes and sausages. Splendid chocolate cake. $$$ 🍷🍷🍷

★★★½ **MAZZEI**—1564 Second Avenue (near 81st Street)—628-3131—Named after an 18th century Italian-American patriot, this cozy trattoria, presided over by Dominic Avelluto and Giuseppe Guglielmi, has developed a loyal following. There's a concise, carefully conceived menu with nightly specials from the wood-burning oven. Baked bocconcini wrapped in prosciutto, sautéed calamari in a tomato sauce, grilled mushrooms, breaded oysters, salmon carpaccio, gnocchi in a wild mushroom sauce, linguine with green beans and peppers, superb Cornish hen with peperoncini, cheesecake, zabaglione. $$$ 🍷🍷

★★ **MEDITERRANEO**—1260 Second Avenue (at 66th Street)—734-7407—A smart-looking trattoria with amiable service, that delivers simple, but very well-executed fare. Swordfish carpaccio, crostini Toscano, grilled portobello mushrooms, pizza rustica (with goat cheese, eggplant and tomato), pizza arrabiata (with spicy salami, tomato and mozzarella) ravioli with gorgonzola, tagliolini al pomodoro, tiramisù. $$½ 🍷🍷

★★½ **MEZZALUNA**—1295 Third Avenue (near 74th Street)—535-9600—Possibly borrowing a note from Melon's next-door, Mezzaluna's walls are decked out with dozens of artful interpretations of the two-handled chopping device after which the restaurant is named. This bristling trattoria is still going strong with a lively crowd. Good carpaccio, insalata Mezzaluna, pumpkin tortelloni, pasta specials and superb brick oven pizzas. No reservations. No credit cards. 🍷

★★★ **MORTIMER'S**—1057 Lexington Avenue (at 75th Street)—517-6400—For years, Mortimer's has reigned supreme as watering hole and eatery of preference for Manhattan glitterati (at midday it virtually functions as a private club for ladies who lunch; it fills with an army of notables by night), and, as a result, non-regulars may be treated with indifference. Food has always been simple and good. Baby Caesar salad, tomato tart, Senegalese soup, twin burgers Mortimer, steak frites, roast chicken, excellent profiteroles. $$$ 🍷🍷

★★★ **ORIENTA**—205 East 75th Street (between Third and Second Avenues)—517-7509—This tiny room is smart, simple and soothing. Flattering light emanates from "coolie" sconces—a motif that is perpetuated in renderings of the restaurant's spunky mascot, a canine sporting a coolie hat. We particularly like the savory starters such as Malaysian chicken satay, Vietnamese spring rolls, vegetarian summer rolls, and pork and leek dumplings. Recommended main courses include chicken curry, pad Thai noodles with shrimp, duck breast with sautéed scallion noodles, coconut crème brûlée, semolina pudding. $$½ 🍷🍷

★★★½ **PAOLA'S RESTAURANT**—347 East 85th Street (near First Avenue)—794-1890—A tiny, convivial and glowing neighborhood spot that is wonderfully intimate for a party of two, yet is surprisingly accommodating for a table of ten. The kitchen is clearly accomplished, and service is smart and unobtrusive. Caesar salad, panzanella, malfatti with Swiss chard, cavatelli with sweet sausages and broccoli di rabe, tortelloni stuffed with veal and chicken, roasted leg of lamb, tiramisù, fresh fruit zabaglione. $$$ 🍷🍷🍷

★½ **PAPAYA KING**—179 East 86th Street (near Third Avenue)—369-0648—Hot dogs and papaya juice may be one of the odder combinations in gastronomy, but it is definitely a New York specialty. The idea was introduced in the late 1920s by a Greek immigrant, and the original Papaya King has been copied by any number of imitators. It's packed with customers who come here to devour the beef franks and the papaya drink made with a little milk and sugar. No reservations. No credit cards. $

★★★★½ **PARIOLI ROMANISSIMO**—24 East 81st Street (near Madison Avenue)—288-2391—This townhouse setting with its subtle tones and tremendous warmth may be the most romantic spot in town. It is presided over by the delightful Rubrio Rossi, whose impeccable attention to detail is always apparent. Our favorite is the front dining room which sports cane-backed chairs, architectural details, flattering lighting, and Rothschild lillies centered on each table. Service is professional and discreet. Fondue of pumpkin soup, baby artichokes filled with minced vegetables, pepper-crusted yellowfin tuna, risotto of the day, breast of guinea hen with chanterelles and potato purée, boneless saddle of venision with chestnut purée, rack of lamb with candied mustard fruits. Leave room for one of the best array of cheeses found anywhere in the city, plus desserts like apple tart, floating island, cheesecake. $$$$$ 🍷🍷🍷

★★½ **PARMA**—1404 Third Avenue (at 79th Street)—535-3520—A neighborhood classic, featuring traditional, if not old-fashioned, Italian fare. The dark paneled setting is quite comforting, and the staff is particularly friendly, greeting regulars and newcomers with equal enthusiasm. It's a perfect place to take the family to savor the likes of grilled porcini mushrooms, pasta malfatti, ravioli stuffed with ricotta and spinach or veal with prosciutto and fontina, veal chop, tantalizing tiramisù and tartufo. $$$ 🍷🍷

★★½ **PETALUMA**—1356 First Avenue (at 73rd Street)—772-8800—This attractive and airy Upper East Side spot has weathered changes in management and in the kitchen, yet remains as popular and inviting as ever. Lots of lightly sauced grilled fare from vegetables to tuna to chicken share the stage alongside brick oven pizza (quatro staggione, a good bet), pasta specials and good omelets. Convenient to nearby Sotheby's. $$½ 🍷🍷

★★★ **THE POLO**—840 Madison Avenue (near 70th Street in the Westbury Hotel)—439-4835—This bland room with paisley banquettes and horsey prints has a lot less personality than talented chef Kerry Heffernan's sparkling cuisine. Unfortunately, his adventurous menu cannot counteract the dull and hotel-like nature of the uninspired staff. Curried cauliflower soup with smoked salmon, sashimi of yellowfin tuna, grilled Louisiana shrimp with artichokes, herb-basted Amish chicken, glazed banana Napoleon, parfait of hazelnuts with coffee anglaise. At lunch, Heffernan's chicken club with pancetta and pickled vegetables is sublime. $$$½ 🍷🍷🍷

★★½ **PORTICO**—1431 Second Avenue (between 74th and 75th Streets)—794-1032—Mauro Chiappe presides over an artfully designed, contemporary-looking trattoria. His staff is friendly and knowledgeable as they present examples of the creative pasta combinations that form part of the ever-changing nightly repertoire. Polenta bruschetta with sautéed zucchini and onions, calamari with mushrooms, grilled 'real' range poussin with herbs and garlic, veal chop Milanese, wonderful home-made desserts. $$$½ 🍷🍷🍷

★★½ **PRIMAVERA**—1578 First Avenue (at 82nd Street)—861-8608—Crowds still flock to this darkly-paneled, clubby establishment, even though the fare can be inconsistent. Some signature dishes like roasted goat can dazzle, and pastas like cavatelli with meat sauce, and penne all'arrabiata can be delicious. The veal chop with porcini is also a good bet. But some nights, similar fare can be disappointing. Extensive but expensive wine list. Dinner only. $$$$ 🍷🍷🍷

★★★★ **QUATORZE bis**—323 East 79th Street (between First and Second Avenues)—535-1414—Quatorze bis brings a bit of the Boulevard Saint Germain to 79th Street. Though the crowd is very Upper East Side, the bistro menu is as authentic as the period poster art which bedecks the dining room. Owners Peter L. Meltzer (no relation to PASSPORT's author) and Mark DiGiulio have created a highly satisfying fusion of traditional and contemporary bistro fare. Duck sausage, chicory with bacon and hot vinaigrette, lobster bisque, chicken grilled with herbs, grilled salmon sauce choron, braised duck, cassoulet, duck confit "notre façon," choucroute garni, killer French fries, hot apple tart, chocolate hazelnut mousse. Succinct but creative wine list. $$$½ 🍷🍷🍷

★★★½ **QUISISANA**—1319 Third Avenue (between 75th and 76th Streets)—879-5000—A glowing and cozy interior bedecked with photos and paintings celebrating Capri. This charming trattoria produces highly sophisticated Sicilian preparations. Owners Andrea Minopolo and Kari and Bepe Desiderio whose families have been in the restaurant business for over half a century, strive to please. Chef Bepe Desiderio has a special touch with seafood. Grilled baby octopus salad, baked eggplant cake over rugola salad, tubettoni with mussels, beans and tomatoes, John Dory baked in a potato crust, fresh cod with basil, breast of chicken in parmesan cheese with sage and peas, baked tiger shrimp with saffron. Leave room for the dolci Caprese such as the sumptuous chocolate almond torte, cheesecake and semifreddo. $$$ 🍷🍷🍷

★★ **THE RIGHT BANK**—822 Madison Avenue (near 69th Street)—737-2811—This basement-level bistro remains one of the few spots where you can catch a simple and inexpensive meal amidst the glitter of Madison Avenue. It is ideal for a quick lunch or a light dinner. Good onion soup, a variety of omelets and salads priced under $10, plus burgers and sandwiches. There's even a pleasant throwback: quiche Lorraine. $$ 🍷

★★ **SANT AMBROEUS**—1000 Madison Avenue (near 79th Street)—570-2211—A stylish trattoria/tea room with a draped ceiling that creates a pavilion-like effect. However smart the decor, savvy diners should bring their own Italian/English dictionary to decipher the menu, as no translations are provided. "Peasant" tomato salad, artichoke hearts with parmesan, risotto with beef glazes, grilled breast of chicken with snap peas. Desserts are a specialty. $$$ 🍷

★★★ **SARABETH'S KITCHEN**—1295 Madison Avenue (near 92nd Street)—410-7335—This attractive, airy tea room is not only a satisfying destination for brunch and lunch, but also for a hearty dinner. Under the direction of the talented Sarabeth Levine, the kitchen produces delectable baked goods along with a variety of egg dishes such as "Goldi Lox." Caesar salad, chicken burrito, corn fettucine, chicken pot pie, roasted salmon with cous cous, blueberry crumb pie, chocolate mousse cake. No reservations. $$½ 🍷🍷

★★½ **SAVANN EST**—181 East 78th Street (between Lexington and Third Avenues)—396-9300—An unpretentious, minimalist interior with an open kitchen and a dining room done up in gray and silver tones. Chef Danforth Houle (ex-River Café and Bouley) and his partner Richard Sandoval feature lots of Asian flavors at this American bistro and grill. Their intention was to fill a niche for imaginative and eclectic food, and they have mostly succeeded. Maine lobster with baby spinach salad, sweet potato frites and Port lemon sauce, duck confit with a warm salad of red lentils and mustard greens, semi-cured Atlantic cod with a ragoût of cranberry beans, grilled leg of lamb with potato-chive purée and red wine–sage sauce, chocolate peppermint tart, molasses cake with stewed prunes and a maple-cinnamon pear sauce. $$$½ 🍷🍷

★★★½ **SETTE MEZZO**—969 Lexington Avenue (near 70th Street)—472-0400—A lively sibling of Vico Madison, and Sette MoMA (q.v.) Sette Mezzo prevails as the trattoria of choice for the Upper East Side smart set; trendy, stylish and always packed with loyal diners. The appealing menu boasts such signature dishes as the eggplant rollatine, fried zucchini, red snapper with balsamic vinegar, and penne with sausage and broccoli di rabe. The flattened veal chop with olives and tomatoes or its breaded counterpart are another must, or consider the pasta specials like orecchiette with tomatoes, and linguine con vongole. Good tiramisù and tartufo. Sophisticated wine list. Reserve in advance. No credit cards. $$$$ 🍷🍷🍷

★★★½ **SISTINA**—1555 Second Avenue (near 80th

Street)—861-7660—The Brothers Bruno run this small Italian dining room with enormous gusto, and the customers have responded accordingly. The best dishes derive from the Brunos' ancestral region, the Amalfi Coast, so ask what the specials are each night and let them guide you to some real treasures. Sausage and broccoli di rabe, pappardelle alla Sistina, pollo alla Sistina IV, Mediterranean fish stew. Some of the best espresso in the city. Well-chosen Italian wine list. Amex only. $$$$ 🍷🍷🍷

★★½ **SOFIA**—1022 Madison Avenue (at 79th Street)—734-2676—An appealing, walk-up trattoria which takes up the second and third floors above a shop, with an unfocused hustle that is redolent of an airport lounge. Service is friendly and the crowd attractive. The menu, however, is somewhat standard, with such offerings as carpaccio and brick oven pizzas, and pastas like linguine with baby clams and penne with sausage, panna cotta, chocolate mousse, pear tart. $$½ 🍷

★★½ **SYRAH**—1400 Second Avenue (between 73rd and 72nd Streets)—327-1780—This restaurant-intensive sector of Second Avenue is distinguished by Syrah's inviting bright red facade and an attractive interior that sports mocha-sponged walls and geometric-patterned banquettes. Chef/owner Ahmed el Sheikh has devised an appealing menu, which is complemented by a wide assortment of wines by the glass, especially the syrah varietal. Radish, watercress and roasted walnut salad, crab meat salad with citrus-beet vinaigrette, sautéed wild mushrooms with goat cheese, swordfish burger, chicken paillard with roasted red peppers, grilled leg of lamb with mushroom sauce and garlic mashed potatoes, sautéed shrimp and scallops with black olives and sun-dried tomatoes, cheesecake. A convenient destination after a hard day's bidding at nearby Sotheby's. Pre-theater dinner $17.95. $$$ 🍷🍷🍷

★★★ **TABLE D'HOTE**—44 East 92nd Street (between Madison and Park Avenues)—348-8125—This tiny white-walled spot is dotted with prints, pottery and mirrors. A smart green plaid dresses up the chairs and banquettes. The relaxed atmosphere recalls the Village more so than Carnegie Hill. Yet the fare is far more sophisticated than the decor suggests. Artichoke soup with fennel, goat cheese salad, wild boar and merguez sausage, seared tuna spring roll with Japanese rice, shrimp with white beans, crispy duck with baked spaghetti squash, apple crumble, ginger brioche pudding, warm chocolate soufflé. $$$½ 🍷🍷

★½ **THE THREE GUYS**—960 Madison Avenue (near 76th Street)—628-8108—This is just a coffee shop—simple and cheap—but it is one of the last vestiges of a Manhattan tradition (à la Mayflower Coffee Shop in the old Savoy Plaza Hotel). Prompt, efficient service. Decent club sandwiches and hamburgers. Attracts the Madison Avenue art set. Recently renovated. $

★★½ **TIRAMISU**—1410 Third Avenue (at 80th Street)—988-9780—Third Avenue has become the land of the wood-oven pizza, but this attractive, brick-walled addition to the strip continues to warrant a stop. In addition to the pizzas (try the alla salsicca), you can also sup on a pleasing array of antipasti like stuzzichini (marinated spicy tomatoes), tortino di carciofi, pasta specials, even Florentine steak. And needless to say, the tiramisù isn't bad either. Good wine list. No credit cards. $$½ 🍷🍷

★★★½ **TROIS JEAN**—154 East 79th Street (near Lexington Avenue)—988-4858—A highly popular, two-story neighborhood bistro which can be lively and fun—so long as the staff's sporadic Gallic hauteur doesn't intervene. The downstairs dining area has been transformed with shiny woods, gleaming glass and an expanded seating area. Presided over by chef Jean-Louis Dumonet, the menu is a satisfying combination of contemporary and traditional French fare, and the wine list is distinctive. Beef consommé with sautéed porcinis and grilled foie gras, salad of haricots verts with walnuts and parmesan, ravioli with snails and spinach, risotto with white truffles, hanger steak, choucroute garni, sautéed sweetbreads and artichokes with cumin, grilled and roasted rack of lamb, chocolate pyramid with raspberry sauce, anise crème brûlée, apple tart. $$$$ 🍷🍷🍷

★★½ **VIVOLO**—140 East 74th Street (at Lexington Avenue)—737-3533—An extremely reasonable approach to wine and food pricing distinguishes this clubby-looking, traditional ristorante. Pre-theater menu is $18.95. After 9:00 PM, there is a $13.95 fixed price menu. A la carte pastas like fettuccine al pesto and entrées such as chicken with tomato and mushroom sauce or veal scallopine all log in under $20. What's more, the kitchen will prepare practically any dish to your specifications. The wine list represents equally good value. In addition, Vivolo now boasts an adjacent café called VIVOLO CUCINA where you can order a delectable sandwich, pasta, or simple salad with a glass of wine or espresso for well under $15. $$½ 🍷🍷🍷

★★½ **VOULEZ VOUS**—1462 First Avenue (at 76th Street)—249-1776—A very pleasant neighborhood bistro with a contemporary look, serving better-than-average French fare. Expect traditional offerings like saucisson de Lyons, rillettes, onion soup, moules marinières, cassoulet, confit of duck, steak au poivre, profiteroles. Open Sunday. Fixed price dinner (with wine) $39.50. $$$ 🍷🍷🍷

★★★½ **WILLOW**—1022 Lexington Avenue (corner 73rd Street)—717-0703—This inviting townhouse setting that has been home to several restaurants over the past decade has been much enlivened by the arrival of Vivek Bundhu and Laurie Gibbons (owners of Table D'Hôte. q.v.). They enlarged the dining area by removing the precarious spiral staircase and gave the walls a warm yellow glow, nicely accented by lamplight. Country flowers and charming paintings create a mood that is cozy and serene. At lunch, there's an array of satisfying sandwiches and salads, plus more sophisticated fare like crispy duck with Savoy cabbage. For dinner, the seasonal menu may include seared sea scallops with chestnut-bean pancakes, pan-roasted quail with mesclun salad, loin of juniper-marinated venison, roasted organic chicken with mashed potatoes, Atlantic salmon with porcini, warm chocolate cake, hot apple crumble, roasted pear with ginger caramel. Sidewalk dining in season. $$$$ 🍷🍷🍷

★★ **ZOCALO**—174 East 82nd Street (between Third and Lexington Avenues)—717-7772—Replacing former occupant Mambo Grill is this glowing, casual restaurant with an open kitchen, ceiling fans, blue-sponged walls and terra cotta pottery. The front bar room (which churns out a good margarita) is more inviting than the back, save for the fact that smoking is permitted. The menu aspires to a somewhat more sophisticated level of cuisine than in standard Mexican eateries. Good salsa, tomatillo, and adobe sauces, queso fundido with chorizo, calamares fritos, fried oysters with chipotle mayonnaise, grilled shrimp in adobo sauce, grilled pork tenderloin tacos, halibut steamed in banana leaves served with rice and beans. $$$ 🍷🍷

SIXTY-SIXTH STREET TO HARLEM (WEST)

★★★½ **222**—222 West 79th Street (near Amsterdam Avenue)—799-0400—The setting is a squeaky clean townhouse replete with new paneling, an assortment of crystal chandeliers and sconces, plus an amusing selection of prints and engravings. Owner Frank Valenza has certainly taken a positive turn with chef Carl Young, whose cuisine is considerably more creative and less expensive than the original manifestation. (Only the very pricey wine list remains out of sync.) Apart from the fact that tables for two can be unbearably cramped, 222 delivers a very enjoyable experience, with an enthusiastic, upbeat staff. Spicy salmon tartare with mascarpone, creamy polenta cakes with wild mushrooms, seared pepper tuna, young Amish free-range chicken with potato purée, dry-aged sirloin steak with horseradish whipped potatoes, prime rack of lamb with white beans, peach cobbler, poached pears. $$$$ 🍷🍷

★★½ **ANSONIA**—329 Columbus Avenue (near 76th Street)—579-0505—Having gone through several manifestations over the years, this space is now an upscale contemporary American restaurant. Unfortunately, the awkward layout hasn't changed, so in order to access the upstairs dining room, you still have to squeeze past a smoky bar packed three-deep and up a long staircase to an overheated balcony with bare tables and a high decibel level. Chef Bill Telepan's (ex Gotham Bar & Grill) modern food is a welcome addition to the neighborhood, but it is quite expensive. Sautéed foie gras with corn, seafood platter, tuna tartare, wild striped bass, lavender-glazed duck, bittersweet chocolate soufflé, peach tart with almonds. $$$$ 🍷🍷🍷

🍎 ★★★½ **CAFÉ DES ARTISTES**—1 West 67th Street (near Central Park West)—877-3500—Despite Howard Chandler Christy's landmark murals of ageless beauties cavorting about the walls, this classic destination

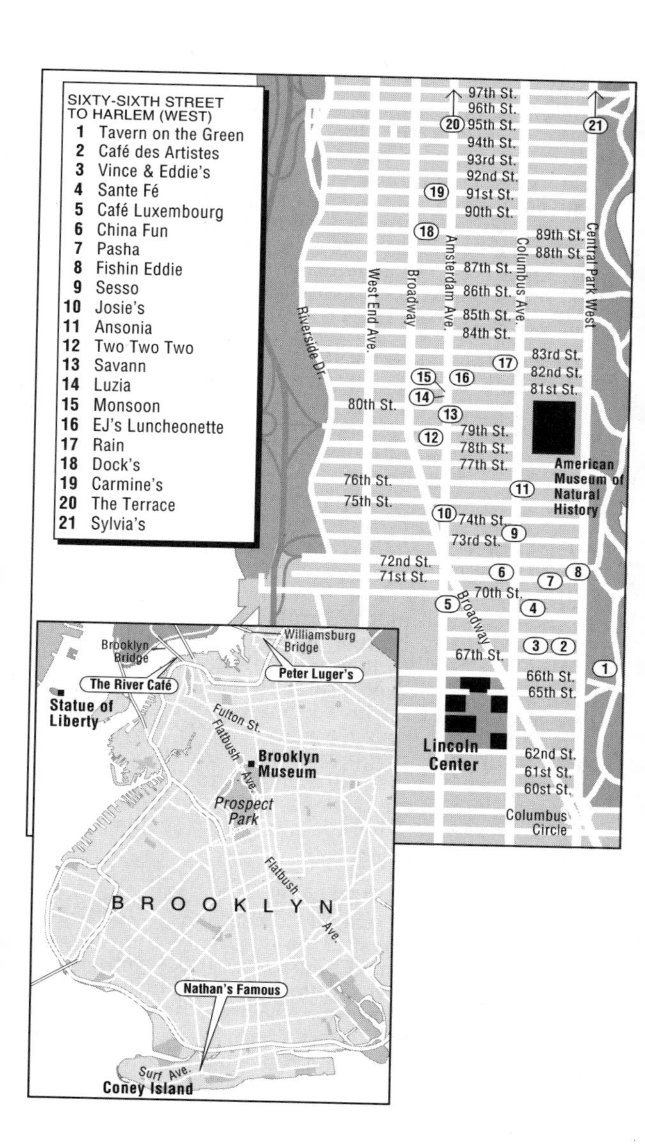
SIXTY-SIXTH STREET TO HARLEM (WEST)
1 Tavern on the Green
2 Café des Artistes
3 Vince & Eddie's
4 Sante Fé
5 Café Luxembourg
6 China Fun
7 Pasha
8 Fishin Eddie
9 Sesso
10 Josie's
11 Ansonia
12 Two Two Two
13 Savann
14 Luzia
15 Monsoon
16 EJ's Luncheonette
17 Rain
18 Dock's
19 Carmine's
20 The Terrace
21 Sylvia's
97th St.
96th St.
95th St.
94th St.
93rd St.
92nd St.
91st St.
90th St.
89th St.
88th St.
87th St.
86th St.
85th St.
84th St.
83rd St.
82nd St.
81st St.
80th St.
79th St.
78th St.
77th St.
76th St.
75th St.
74th St.
73rd St.
72nd St.
71st St.
70th St.
67th St.
66th St.
65th St.
62nd St.
61st St.
60st St.
Riverside Dr.
West End Ave.
Broadway
Amsterdam Ave.
Columbus Ave.
Central Park West
American Museum of Natural History
Lincoln Center
Columbus Circle
Brooklyn Bridge
Williamsburg Bridge
Peter Luger's
The River Café
Statue of Liberty
Fulton St.
Flatbush Ave.
Brooklyn Museum
Prospect Park
BROOKLYN
Nathan's Famous
Surf Ave.
Coney Island

seems to have lost a bit of its vitality. The rooms retain a certain charm—abundant floral displays, deep green banquettes, a warm patina and dark wood trim. But the greeting is indifferent, and service is somber and stiff. Owners George and Jenifer Lang have devised an eclectic menu, with starters such as black bean soup, country paté, and snails in creamy garlic sauce. Hearty main courses include Austrian beef goulash, duck confit with white beans, bourride with aioli. This has always been a favorite stop for desserts like the Illona tart, mocha dachoise, chocolate peanut butter candy bar mousse cake. Original selection of house wines priced at $20. Fixed price $19.97 lunch. $$$$$ 🍷🍷🍷

★★★ **CAFÉ LUXEMBOURG**—200 West 70th Street (near Amsterdam Avenue)—873-7411—A West Side institution, this handsome space with a popular bar is a casual and stylish outpost for late night dining. Bistro fare can be quite creative here. Potato and fennel vichyssoise, steak frites, duck breast with apples, profiteroles with white chocolate mint chip ice cream. $$$ 🍷🍷🍷

★★ **CARMINE'S**—2450 Broadway (near 91st Street)—362-2200—Those who wouldn't deign to set foot in Little Italy or have never eaten in the Bronx, Brooklyn or Queens, have made Carmine's a retro-chic restaurant of daunting popularity—a big, sprawling, loud, red-sauce, family place with old-fashioned Italian-American food served in double portions at very fair prices. Not that Carmine's is any better than dozens of other Italian-American restaurants in NYC; people wait an hour or more to gorge here on rubbery calamari, very good pastas, and nice, garlicky chicken scarpariello. Volume business means volume cooking and slow service. There is a branch transplant in the Theater District. $$½ 🍷

★★★ **CHINA FUN RESTAURANT**—246 Columbus Avenue (between 71st and 72nd Streets)—580-5298—The West Side outpost of the Second Avenue flagship (q.v.) proffers original Chinese fare in a simple, sleek, high-tech setting where you can watch the professional kitchen team in action. Wonton soup, dim sum, steamed short ribs in black bean sauce, fried stuffed crab claws, grilled vegetable stick, hot and spicy Chinese baby eggplant, lemon chicken, kung po scallops. There are two dozen lunch-time specials priced under $5.00 which come with soup or an egg roll, rice and fruit. $$ 🍷

★★½ **DOCK'S**—2427 Broadway, (near 89th Street)—724-5588—This is a highly popular spot for seafood, contemporary in look but with the charm of an old-time seafood house. You dine on two separate levels separated by stairs and a gleaming brass rail. A blackboard lists the daily oyster specials, along with the catch of the day (which will also be rhymed off by your waiter.) Count on staples such as Caesar salad, grilled scallops, salmon, and halibut, plus desserts like chocolate mud cake and key lime pie. Fixed price brunch $12.50. $$$ 🍷🍷

★★ **EJ'S LUNCHEONETTE**—477 Amsterdam Avenue (between 81st and 82nd Streets)—873-3444—A popular West Side spot (with an East Side sibling, q.v.) for a reasonably priced family breakfast, brunch, lunch or dinner. The interior decor is kitsch without being in any way contrived, and the menu, though simple, is well executed. A wide array of breakfast dishes includes flapjacks, waffles, and eggs galore. Lunch or dinner consists of a broad selection of sandwiches, burgers and salads, some designed for the health conscious. You can order a traditional turkey club sandwich or opt for the EJ version, made with avocado and chicken. There are also daily specials, soups and salads. Don't overlook the addictive French fries, milk shakes and malteds. No reservations. No credit cards. $$ 🍷

★★ **FISHIN EDDIE**—73 West 71st Street (near Columbus Avenue)—874-3474—With a seeming lack of finesse but a canny sense of the market, Fishin Eddie established itself upon opening as the most popular seafood house on Manhattan's Upper West Side, on the coattails of older sibling, Vince & Eddie's (q.v.). The premises look deliberately ramshackle, like an old seafood house in Montauk or the Cape. Seafood is handled impeccably here, though the rest of the food and desserts (go with the biscotti) are not up to the same standard. Steamed Dungeness crab, linguine marinara, grilled yellowfin tuna, sole à la meunière. $$½ 🍷🍷

★★ **JOSIE'S**—300 Amsterdam Avenue (corner 74th Street)—769-1212—An undulating zinc bar, potted plants and ceiling fans are the setting for this relaxed and breezy vegetarian/organic restaurant. Even the provenance of all poultry and meats served here is identified on the menu in order to demonstrate that an item is free-range or fat-free. Some vegetarian items like the faux "sushi" roll with portabello mushrooms, and roasted eggplant cake are quite appealing. The ginger grilled calamari with salsa was another winner, but the grilled breast of chicken with sliced portobello mushrooms, and the marinated steak fajita need work. $$½ 🍷🍷

★★½ **LUZIA**—429 Amsterdam Avenue (between 80th and 81st Streets)—595-2000—Recently renovated, this diminutive space with brick and tiled walls sports a friendly and relaxed air. Portuguese sausage is grilled tableside. Clams or mussels Portuguese style come in phyllo dough with spinach and feta. The signature dish here is Portuguese fish stew. Also worth considering are chicken in Port wine, baked ham with pineapple glaze, braised brisket of beef. For dessert, there's Luzia's chocolate cake, and white chocolate mousse cake. Take-out as well. $$ 🍷

★★ **MONSOON**—435 Amsterdam Avenue (at 81st Street)—580-8686—This low-key Vietnamese restaurant draws high-volume customers who have been known to line up even in driving rain for a table. (Reservations are only taken for parties of seven or more.) The fare is authentic, though somewhat lacking in finesse, with appetizers outshining main course dishes. Vietnamese spring roll, BBQ beef satés, shrimp dumpling in red miso shrimp sauce, curry chicken with eggplant, stir-fried noodles, cream caramel custard. $$ 🍷

★★½ **PASHA**—70 West 71st Street (between Columbus Avenue and Central Park West)—579-8751—You enter a comely front atrium only to be ushered into a rather simple white dining room with Turkish works of art. This is a very homey spot with food prepared from family recipes, not just the usual collection of kabobs. The appetizers are particularly savory, and prices are moderate enough to allow ample tastes. Crispy calamari with garlic-walnut sauce, baby stuffed eggplant, steamed lamb dumplings, marinated swordfish, braised lamb shank, poached apricots. The wine list has a couple of interesting Turkish wines. $$$ 🍷

★★½ **RAIN**—100 West 82nd Street (near Columbus Avenue)—501-0776—This is a smart space with stenciled floors, shadow boxes, festive silks, wooden banquettes, and colorful rattan in the bar area. The eclectic Asian menu incorporates the cuisines of Thailand, Malaysia and Vietnam. Crispy Vietnamese spring rolls, roti (Malaysian flat bread) with curry, Thai-style crab cakes, spicy stir-fried jumbo shrimp with bamboo shoots, Thai dumplings, sautéed cashew chicken. Good selection of wines by the glass, good beer list. $$ 🍷🍷

★★½ **SANTA FÉ**—72 West 69th Street (near Columbus Avenue)—724-0822—A forerunner of the trendy South-West/Tex-Mex eateries which have since invaded Manhattan, this cozy and surprisingly peaceful place, with its peach colored interior, is still going strong. Good salsa, quesadilla, ceviche with avocado and peppers, Southwestern pork chops with jalapeño jelly, Yucatan chicken with puréed smoked chili peppers, tacos al carbon, apple crisp. $$½ 🍷

★★½ **SAVANN**—414 Amsterdam Avenue (between 79th and 80th Streets)—580-0202—A compact and dimly-lit spot with brick and sponged walls, oversized gilded mirrors, and a lively, casually clad crowd. The menu abounds with basic American fare, with the occasional Asian borrowing evidenced in a profusion of dumplings. Hot and sour wild mushroom soup with vegetable dumplings, grilled portabello mushroom, steamed shrimp dumplings, grilled chicken breast with chive potato purée, hangar steak in red wine sauce, chocolate covered mousse cake, caramel banana Napoleon with praline ice cream. $$$½ 🍷🍷

★★½ **SESSO**—285 Columbus Avenue (between 73rd and 74th Streets)—501-0607—You drink downstairs but dine upstairs, surrounded by bright orange walls, red chairs, blue-tiled tables and flickering votive candles. Chef Erica Miller's menu is as varied as the restaurant's color scheme. Her food is hearty and portions are generous, with an emphasis on value. Steamed mussels with Pernod, goat cheese soufflé, cornish hen, peppered tuna, vegetable Napoleon, crème brûlée, "chocolate, chocolate, chocolate." $$½ 🍷

★★½ **SYLVIA'S**—328 Lenox Avenue (near 126th Street)—996-0660—If you're craving great barbecue, downhome soul food, and something uniquely New York, catch a cab up to Harlem to Sylvia's, a marvelous restaurant serving up batches of great ribs, pork chops, candied sweet potatoes, and pecan pies that will satisfy the biggest eater in family. Service is warm and friendly. Amex only. $$½ 🍷

○ ★★½ **TAVERN ON THE GREEN**—67th Street and Central Park West—873-3200—This is certainly one of the original "theme" restaurants, conceived by the flamboyant Warner Leroy long before the genre became gospel. With its fantasy of lights and kitsch, this is a festive oasis for out-of-town diners who are truly delighted to be here. (There is more magic to the wedding cake atmosphere at night.) Chef Patrick Clark delivers a serious boost to this high-volume kitchen. But due to the crowds, service tends to be more polite than proficient, and the menu reads better than it tastes. Shrimp and corn dumplings, Caesar salad and parmesan crisps, char-grilled tuna with avocado salad, Moroccan style barbecued salmon, cheesecake, banana split. Fixed price lunch is $26. Pre-theater dinner is $22.50 to $28.50. $$$$ 🍷🍷🍷

★★★½ **THE TERRACE**—400 West 119th Street (near Amsterdam Avenue)—666-9490—This uptown space, with its panoramic view of Manhattan and the Hudson River, is unfamiliar to many New Yorkers. It's an ideal spot for a festive outing, rife with romance. Chef Kenny Johnson has now elevated the food to new heights with his eclectic menu. Yellowfin tuna carpaccio with Asian salad, fricassée of escargot with apple-smoked bacon, pepper-crusted Hudson Valley foie gras, sliced breast of Muscovy duck with apple-potato rosti, oven-roasted veal chop with onion-potato galette, strawberries with Tahitian vanilla gelato, frozen caramel mousse gateau. $$$$$ 🍷🍷🍷

★★½ **VINCE & EDDIE'S**—70 West 68th Street (between Central Park West and Columbus Avenue)—721-0068—Named after original owners Vincent Orgera and Eddie Schoenfeld (who has since left), this place hasn't looked back since its successful debut. The attractive, modified country look was orchestrated by the late Sam Lopata. The menu is succinct and fairly reasonably priced, Crisp calamari with cilantro lime sauce, Chesapeake crabcakes with sauce diablo, coriander crusted tuna, grilled sirloin and steak fries, homemade ice creams. Garden dining in season. $$$½ 🍷🍷

BROOKLYN

○ ★½ **NATHAN'S FAMOUS**—1315 Surf Avenue (at Stillwell Avenue)—718-946-2202—This is a grand institution, as old as the Brooklyn Dodgers but obviously more durable. Nathan Handwerker didn't invent the hot dog, but he did more to popularize it than anyone else, and it's still a nonpareil frank. The Coney Island location has nostalgia on its side. $

○ ★★★ **PETER LUGER**—178 Broadway (Brooklyn)—718-387-7400—If you are curious about experiencing a taste of 19th-century New York, then a visit to Peter Luger (opened in 1887) justifies the trek to this historic sector of Brooklyn. The Teutonic chop-house look—with roughly hewn refectory tables and beer steins for decoration—has its charm, and so do the deliberately brusque waiters. The menu offers little choice—tomato and onion salad, sensational Porterhouse ($57 for two is a relative bargain by Manhattan standards), lamb chops, an enormous portion of French fries, bland creamed spinach, cheesecake. You can experience it all for a fraction of the price at lunch time when $7.95 specials are the norm. Nonetheless, Peter Luger is more than just a curiosity, especially for committed carnivores. $$$$½ 🍷

○ ★★★½ **THE RIVER CAFE**—1 Water Street (under the Brooklyn Bridge)—718-522-5200—Day or night, the majestic view from The River Cafe of the Manhattan cityscape is positively breathtaking, and this continues to be one of the "must-go" restaurants that defines NYC's unique grandeur. From its inception, the Cafe has also been a laboratory for eclectic cooking under a series of brilliant young chefs who have gone on to their own stellar restaurants. Presently, the executive chef is Rick Laakkonen, who is a master of presentation and execution, without falling prey to the eccentricity of some of his predecessors. Tuna and salmon tartare, sweetbreads and lemon tagliarini, terrine of smoked duck foie gras, pan-roasted monkfish with chanterelles, filet of pork with potato and leek purée, pan-roasted rabbit with ricotta canelloni, warm apple tart, caramelized pear and frangipan tart, hot chocolate soufflé. Fixed price dinner $68. 🍷🍷🍷🍷

FOOD DICTIONARY

FRENCH

Aiguillettes de canard—duck breasts
Aïoli—a garlic mayonnaise
Ananas—pineapple
Béchamel—a white, milk-based sauce
Beurre blanc—"white butter" sauce
Beurre noir—"black butter," a cooked brown butter sauce
Boeuf à la bourguignonne—beef stew cooked in red wine
Bordelaise—a demiglace and red wine sauce with parsley and shallots
Bouillabaisse—Marseilles seafood stew
Bourride—provençal fish stew with garlic mayonnaise
Brandade de morue—pureed cod, garlic and potatoes
Cassis—black currant
Cassoulet—dish of beans, pork, preserved duck, sausage and seasonings
Cerise—cherry
Chanterelle—wild mushroom shaped like small trumpet
Chantilly—served with lightly whipped cream
Chevreuil—venison
Choucroute garni—smoked pork, sausage, preserved duck and sauerkraut
Civet—stew
Citron—lemon
Confit de canard—duck meat preserved in its own fat
Confiture—a jam-like reduction of fruit or vegetables
Crème à l'anglaise—a thickened custard sauce
Crème brûlée—dessert custard with a burned sugar crust
Daube—braised meat
Dijonnaise—mustard sauce
Duxelles—minced mushrooms
Écrevisse—crayfish
En gelée—in jellied aspic
Espadon—swordfish
Faisan—pheasant
Farci—stuffed
Financière—with mushrooms, Madeira and truffles
Forestière—cooked with mushrooms
Fraîche—fresh
Frisée—curly leaf lettuce
Fruits de mer—seafood
Galette—a small cake
Grand veneur—"hunter style," with red wine, cream and currant jelly
Grillade—grilled meat
Ile flottante—"Floating island" meringues in custard
Italienne—demiglace flavored with tomato and bacon
Langoustine—large shrimp
Lapin—rabbit
Lardon—bacon
Lentilles—lentils
Mâche—lamb's lettuce
Maïs—corn
Marjolaine—a richly textured chocolate and hazelnut cake
Mesclun—mixed wildgreens

Meunière—fish cooked in butter and lemon
Mille-feuille—puff pastry
Morille—wild mushroom, morel
Mornay—béchamel sauce enriched with cheese
Moules—mussels
Navarin—lamb stew
Nouilles—noodles
Oursin—sea urchin
Pâté—forcemeat cut in slabs
Pâte—pastry
Périgourdine—demiglace sauce with truffles
Pied-de-porc—pig's feet
Pintadeau—guinea hen
Poireaux—leeks
Poivre vert—green pepper
Pommes—apples
Poularde—large roasting chicken
Poussin—young chicken
Praline—caramelized, pulverized almonds
Raie—skate
Ravigote—vinegar-based caper, onion and herbs sauce
Rémoulade—mayo flavored with mustard and gherkins and anchovy essence
Rillettes—pork or goose mashed with fat
Ris de veau—veal sweetbreads
Rognon—kidney
Rouget—red mullet
Saint-Pierre—John Dory fish
Suprême de volaille—boneless breast of chicken, sautéed in butter
Tarte Tatin—hot apple tart
Thon—tuna
Tripes à la mode de Caen—tripe cooked in an onion, bacon and garlic sauce
Vacherin—meringue dessert with ice cream layers
Vol-au-vent—flaky pastry shell

GREEK

Armi—lamb
Baklava—sweet flakey phyllo pastry
Dolma—stuffed grape leaves
Hummos—creamy chick pea and tahini puree
Keftedhes—seasoned meatballs
Mezze—appetizer
Psomi—bread
Taramasalata—appetizer dip of mashed cod roe

INDIAN

Aloo chat—potatoes cooked with spices
Biryani—fragrant rice dishes
Dal—lentil-based side dish
Dosa—a stuffed crepe
Gobhi—cabbage or cauliflower
Gosht do piaz—meat and onion stew
Jalebi—swirls of deep-fried batter in sugar syrup
Keema—ground meat dish
Kheer—rice cooked in milk
Kofta—meatballs
Korma—braised meat and yogurt dishes
Kulfi—ice cream with nuts
Matar paneer—spicy side dish of cheese and vegetables
Murgh—chicken
Pakoras—deep-fried vegetable dumplings
Ras malai—cheese dessert
Shorba—soup
Vindaloo—a spicy hot lamb dish

ITALIAN

Abbachio—very young lamb
Acciuga—anchovies
Aglio e olio—garlic and oil
Amatriciana—sauce of tomatoes, hot peppers and pancetta ham
Arrabbiata—a freshly-made tomato and hot pepper pasta sauce
Baccalà—salted dried cod
Bagna cauda—anchovies, garlic and pepper in which vegetables are cooked or dipped
Bocconcini—balls of mozzarella or veal
Bollito misto—boiled mixed meats
Bresaola—dried beef
Brodetto—fish soup
Bruschetta—toasted Italian bread, often with garlic and tomato
Bucatini—tubular pasta
Capellini—very thin spaghetti
Caponata—a hot, spicy, eggplant and pepper marinade
Cappesante—scallops
Capro—goat
Carciofi—artichokes
Casalinga—"homestyle" food
Cipolla—onion
Coniglio—rabbit
Costoletta—cutlet
Cotechino—large pork sausage
Cozze—mussels
Fegato—liver
Fichi—figs
Finocchio—fennel
Focaccia—puffy, pizza-like bread, often sprinkled with rosemary
Fragole—strawberries
Fritto—fried
Frutti di mare—mixed seafood
Gamberi—shrimp
Gelati—ice creams
Gnocchi—potato dumplings
Grissini—breadsticks
Lenticchie—lentils
Lepre—hare
Lumache—snails
Mascarpone—a rich butter-like cheese
Melanzana—eggplant
Orecchiette—ear-shaped pasta
Ostriche—oysters
Pappardelle—flat wide pasta, sometimes shaped like butterflies
Pesto—basil, garlic, pignoli and olive oil sauce
Pignoli—pine nuts
Piselli—peas
Polenta—cooked cornmeal
Polpo—octopus
Primavera—"springtime," refers to dishes with vegetables
Puttanesca—a robust, spicy tomato and herb sauce
Radicchio—red-leafed bitter lettuce
Ragù—meat and vegetable tomato-based sauce
Risotto—cooked rice dish with other ingredients
Sarde—sardines
Tagliarini—thin spaghetti
Tagliatelle—similar to fettuccine
Tiramisù—mascarpone, espresso and lady finger's dessert
Tonno—tuna
Trippa—tripe
Vitello tonnato—cold veal in creamy tuna sauce

Vongole—clams

Zuppa inglese—sponge cake doused with liqueurs and rum

JAPANESE

Daikon—white radish

Miso—red bean paste

Nori—sheets of black seaweed

Somen—fine noodles

Tatami room—private dining room

Tonkatsu—breaded pork cutlet

Wasabi—very pungent green horseradish

Yosenabe—beef, chicken and vegetables simmered in stock with noodles

KOREAN

Bolgogi—marinated barbecued beef

Kalbee—marinated spareribs

Kimchee—fiery hot chili condiment

Shinsonro—meat, seafood and seaweed casserole

MEXICAN

Carne asado—Mexican pot roast

Chalupas—little pastry "boats" with ground meat

Chiles rellenos—stuffed chile peppers

Mole—creamy sauce often flavored with bitter chocolate

Tamales—corn husk steamed with seasonings

RUSSIAN

Basturma—marinated barbecued beef

Blini—thin buckwheat pancakes

Borsch—beet soup

Pelmeny—Russian ravioli

Piroshkis—stuffed pastries

Varenyky—dessert dumplings

SPANISH

Almejas—clams

Arroz con pollo—rice and chicken dish

Bacalao—salted dried cod

Budín—pudding

Calamar—squid

Lomo—roast pork

Mariscos—shellfish

Tapas—Spanish finger food

Zarzuela—shellfish stew

THAI

Kaeng masaman—chicken or beef curry

Mee krob—crisp-fried noodles with shrimp and egg

Nam pla—fermented fish sauce

Tom yam kong—lemon grass-chili soup

FOOD INDEX

CONTINENTAL

Edwardian Room
540 Park
Rainbow Room, The
Sardi's
Tavern on The Green
World Yacht Cruises
Right Bank, The
River Café, The
Sign of The Dove
Soho Kitchen & Bar
South Street Seaport
Windows on the World
Zoë

DELICATESSEN

Carnegie Deli
Katz's Delicatessen

ECLECTIC

Bar 6
Blue Ribbon
C3
Café 44
Café Botanico
Café Nosidam
Candela
Cub Room
Demi
Duane Park
EJ's Luncheonette
Ed Sullivan's
Fred's
Hot Tomato
Indigo
Jerry's
La Maison Japonaise
Lola
Lobster Club
Kitchen Club
Library, The
Match
Odeon, The
Park Avalon
Park Avenue Café
Pelago
Planet Hollywood
Redeye Grill

FRENCH BISTRO

Bistro de Maxim
Bistro du Nord
Café Luxembourg
Chelsea Bistro & Bar
Chez Jacqueline
Chez Josephine
Chez Michallet
Demarchelier
Dix et Sept
Félix
Ferrier
Frontière
Jean-Claude
Jean Lafitte
JoJo
Jour et Nuit
Jubilée
Jules
L'Absinthe
L'Ardoise
La Colombe D'Or
La Goulue
La Mangeoire
La Table des Rois
Le Bilboquet
Le Pescadou
Le Petit Hulot
Le Réfuge
Le Relais
Le Taxi
Le Zoo
Les Halles
Madame Romaine de Lyons
Opaline
Park Bistro
Pitchoune
Quatorze Bis
Raoul's
Sanzin
Trois Jean
Un Deux Trois
Voulez-Vous

FRENCH DELUXE

Bouterin
Box Tree, The
Café des Artistes
Chanterelle
Daniel
La Caravelle
La Côte Basque
La Grenouille
La Métairie
La Réserve
Le Bernardin
Le Chantilly
Le Périgord
Le Régence
Les Célébrités
Lespinasse
Lutèce
Peacock Alley
Restaurant Raphaël

FILIPINO

Cendrillon

GREEK

Eros
Ithaka
Meltemi
Periyali

ICE CREAM

Serendipity

ITALIAN RISTORANTI

Artusi
Barbetta
Campagna
Felidia
Follonico
Fresco
Girasole
Giovanni
Harry Cipriani
Il Cantinori
Il Cortile
Il Monello
Il Mulino
Il Nido
Le Madri
Letizia
Osteria del Circo
Parioli Romanissimo
Primavera
Remi
San Domenico
San Pietro
Sistina
Vivolo

ITALIAN TRATTORIA

Amici Miei
Angelo's
Arqua
Azzurro
Baoranda
Bar Pitti
Barolo
Bella Blu
Bice
Brio
Caffe Bondí
Carmine's
Cent'Anni
Cellini
Cibo
Cinque Terre
Coco Pazzo
Coco Pazzo Teatro
Col Legno
Contrapunto
Da Ciro
Da Silvano
Da Umberto
Downtown
Elaine's
Elio's
Ennio & Michael
Erminia
Ferrara
Frico Bar
Gabriel
Gigino
Gino
Grand Ticino, The
Hosteria Fiorella
I Trulli
Il Bagatto
Il Buco
Il Toscanaccio
Il Vigneto
John's of Bleecker
Leda
Limoncello
Lumi
Lusardi's
Mangia e Bevi
Mazzei
Meditteraneo
Mezzaluna
Novita
Orso
Osteria al Doge
Paola's
Patsy's
Parma
Petaluma
Pō
Portico
Quisisana
Sant Ambroeus
Savore
Scalinatella
Sette Mezzo
Sette MoMA
SPQR
Sofia
Spartina
Tiramisu
Trattoria Dell'Arte
Tucci
Torre di Pisa
Toscana
Via Oreta
Vico Madison
Yellowfingers
Zona del Chianti
Zeppole

INDIAN

Bombay Palace
Bay Leaf
Dawat
Salaam Bombay

JAPANESE

Honmura An
Hatsuhana
Kuruma Zushi
Nippon
Nobu
Omen
Otabe
Sushi-Say
Takesushi

JEWISH

Katz's Delicatessen

KOREAN

Mirezi
Hangawi

LATIN AMERICAN

Bistro Latino
Circus
Erizo Latino
Patria
Riodizio

MALAYSIAN

Penang

MEDITERRANEAN/ PROVENCAL

Alison on Dominick
Café Centro
Café Crocodile
Capsouto Frères
Matthew's
Montrachet
Picholine
Provence
TriBeCa Grill
Union Square Café
Zucca

MEXICAN

El Teddy's
Mi Cocina
Rosa Mexicano
Zarela
Zocalo

MOROCCAN

Mezze

MIDDLE EASTERN

Al Bustan
Layla

PAN-ASIAN

Rain
Orienta

PORTUGUESE

Luzia

RUSSIAN

Firebird
Pravda

SCANDINAVIAN

Aquavit
Christer's

SEAFOOD

Aqua Grill
Blue Water Grill
Captain's Table
Café Lure
City Crab
Dock's
Fishin Eddie
Grand Central Oyster Bar
Le Bernardin
Le Pescadou
Manhattan Ocean Club
Oceana
Pisces
Sea Grill
Tropica
Water Club, The

SPANISH

Bolo
El Parador
Marichu
Sevilla
Solera
Tapas Lounge

STEAK

Angelo & Maxie's
Ben Benson's
Bruno's Pen & Pencil
Charlton's
Gallagher's
Keen's
Maloney & Porcelli
Old Homestead, The
Palm
Peter Luger
Pietro's
Ruth's Chris Steak House
Smith & Wollensky
Soho Steak
Sparks Steak House
West 63rd Street Steakhouse

THAI

Cha Yen
Puket
Typhoon Brewery
Vong

TURKISH

Deniz
Pasha

VEGETARIAN/ ORGANIC

Josie's

VIETNAMESE

Indochine
Le Colonial
Monsoon

STAR RATINGS

★★★★★
Aureole
Daniel
Felidia
Four Seasons, The
Le Bernardin
Les Célébrités
Lespinasse

★★★★½
Arcadia
Gotham Bar and Grill
JoJo
La Caravelle
Lutèce
March
Montrachet
Oceana
Parioli Romanissimo
Picholine
San Domenico
Union Square Café

★★★★
Alison on Dominick
An American Place
Aquavit
Barbetta
Bouterin
Café Crocodile
Campagna
Cascabel
Chanterelle
Christer's
Dawat
Ennio & Michael
Follonico
Gramercy Tavern
Hangawai
Honmura An
I Trulli
Il Monello
Il Mulino
Il Nido
Kuruma Zushi
L'Absinthe
La Côte Basque
La Goulue
La Grenouille
Le Chantilly
Le Périgord
Lola
Manhattan Ocean Club
Matthew's
Nobu
Osteria del Circo
Pō
Park Avenue Café
Park Bistro
Patria
Peacock Alley
Quatorze bis
Remi
Restaurant Raphael
San Pietro
Sea Grill
Shun Lee Palace
Smith & Wollensky
Solera
Sparks Steak House
Verbena
Vong

★★★½
"21" Club
222
Aqua Grill
Arizona 206
Artusi
Bar Pitti
Bay Leaf Indian Restaurant
Becco
Ben Benson's
Bistro Latino
Bolo
Bombay Palace
Bruno's Pen & Pencil
Café 44
Café des Artistes
Capsouto Frères
Cendrillon
Charlton's
Cinque Terre
Da Umberto
Duane Park Café
Etats Unis
Firebird
Fresco
Gallagher's
Grand Central Oyster Bar
Harry Cipriani
Hudson River Club
Il Cantinori
Jean-Claude
Judson Grill
Keen's
La Métairie
La Mangeoire
Layla
Le Madri
Le Réfuge
Le Régence
Lenox Room, The

Limoncello
Lobster Club
Luma
Maloney & Porcelli
Marguery Grill
Mazzei
Mesa Grill
Monkey Bar
Orso
Palm
Paola's Restaurant
Patroon
Post House, The
Provence
Quilty's
Quisisana
River Café, The
Sanzin
Savoy
Scalinatella
Sette Mezzo
Sign of The Dove
Sistina
Spartina
Sushi-Say
Tapika
Terrace, The
Tribeca Grill
Trois Jean
Willow
Zoë

★★★

5757
Acme Bar & Grill
Aja
Al Bustan
Alva
Arqua
Bella Blu
Bistro de Maxim's
Butterfield 81
Café Botanico
Café Centro
Café Evergreen
Café Luxembourg
Caffe Bondí
Canal House
Captain's Table
Caviarteria
Cellini
Chelsea Bistro & Bar
Chin Chin
China Fun
China Fun Restaurant
China Grill
Circus
Cité
City Wine & Cigar Co.
Coco Pazzo
Coco Pazzo Teatro
Col Legno
Cub Room
Da Ciro
Da Silvano
Edwardian Room, The
Elio's
Félix
Ferrier
Frico Bar
Gabriel
Gigino
Il Toscanaccio
Independent, The
Indigo
La Colombe D'Or
La Réserve
Le Pescadou
Le Petit Hulot
Le Zoo
Leda
Letizia
Lumi
Mesa City
Mezze
Michael's
Mirezi
Mortimer's
Nippon
Novita
Oak Room and Bar, The
Old Homestead, The
Opaline
Patsy's
Pelago
Periyali
Peter Luger
Petrossian
Pietro's
Polo, The
Rosa Mexicano
Rusty Staub's on Fifth
Ruth's Chris Steak House
Sarabeth's Kitchen
Savore
Sevilla
Shun Lee Dynasty
Sweet Ophelia's
Table d'Hôte
Takesushi
Torre di Pisa
Toscana
Tropica
Tse Yang
Typhoon Brewery
Water Club, The
Windows on the World
Zarela
Zen Palate
Zeppole
Zucca

OPEN LATE

(Reservations accepted until 11:00 PM)

Acme Bar & Grill
Alva
Angelo & Maxie's
Ansonia
B. Smith's
Bar Pitti
Barolo
Bella Blue
Bistro du Nord
Bistro Latino
Bolo
Café Beulah
Café des Artistes
Café Lure
Candela
Carmine's
Cha Yen
Chez Josephine
China Fun
Circus
Cité
City Wine & Cigar
Coco Pazzo
Coco Pazzo Teatro
Contrapunto
Club Macanudo
Cub Room
Downtown
Elio's
Erizo Latino
Eros
Felidia
Félix
Ferrier
Firebird
Frico Bar
Gallagher's
Il Buco
Independent
Jean-Claude
Josie's
Judson Grill
Jules
La Goulue
Le Colonial
Le Pescadou
Les Halles
Limoncello
Lola
Lumi
Maloney & Porcelli
Mangia e Bevi
Matthew's
Mesa City
Opaline
Orienta
Pō
Patria
Petrossian
Picholine
Pitchoune
Quatorze Bis
Quilty's
Rain
Rainbow Room, The
Redeye Grill
Rosa Mexicano
San Domenico
Sanzin
Shun Lee
Sofia
Soho Kitchen and Bar
Soho Steak
Tapas Lounge
Tompkins 131
TriBeCa Grill
Trois Jean
Un Deux Trois
Virgil's Barbecue

OPEN AFTER MIDNIGHT

Bar 6
Blue Ribbon
Café Luxembourg
Cité (Grill)
Contrapunto
Elaine's
Empire Diner (24 hours)
Hard Rock Café
Harley Davidson Café
Hot Tomato
Indochine
J.G. Melon's
Jim McMullen
Joe Allen
Jour et Nuit
Lucky Strike
Match
Mezzaluna
Odeon, The
P.J. Clarke's
Park Avalon
Pravda
Sweet Ophelia
Yellowfingers

SUNDAY SUGGESTIONS

BRUNCH & DINNER

5757
Al Bustan
American Festival Café
Aqua Grill
Bar 6
Becco
Bistro du Nord
Café Botanico
Café des Artistes
Café Luxembourg
Capsuoto Frères
Carmine's
Cendrillon
China Fun
Coco Pazzo
Da Silvano
Demi
Downtown
Erizo Latino
Gino
Harley Davidson Café
Harry Cipriani
Home
Hosteria Fiorella
Il Bagatto
Josie's
Kiosk
La Goulue
La Métairie
Le Pescadou
Le Zoo
Lola
Lumi
Mangia e Bevi
Matthew's
Mesa City
Mesa Grill
Old Homestead
Pō
Pisces
Provence
Quisisana
Remi
River Café
Santa Fé
Shun Lee Dynasty
Sign of the Dove
Smith & Wollensky
Syrah
Table d'Hôte
Tapika
Tavern on the Green
The Independent
Tompkins 131
Tribeca Grill
Verbena
Vong
Willow
Zen Palate
Zoë
Zucca

BRUNCH ONLY

Café Beulah
Chez Michallet
Hudson River Club
Jerry's
Lenox Room
Lespinasse
Odeon
Sesso

DINNER ONLY

Bella Blu
Bolo
Bouterin
Butterfield 81
Campagna
Circus
Cité
Cub Room
Dawat
Elio's
Firebird
Gotham Bar & Grill
Il Buco
Il Cantinori
Il Monello
Jean-Claude
Layla
Le Colonial
Le Madri
Lobster Club
Lusardi's
Manhattan Ocean Club
Marguery Grill
Mazzei
Mortimer's
Nobu
Omen
Orienta
Osteria del Circo
Rosa Mexicano
Park Bistro
Quatorze bis
Quilty's
Rain
Rainbow Room
San Domenico
Sanzin
Savoy
Smith & Wollensky
Sette Mezzo
Virgil's Barbecue
Vong

DESTINATION DINING

BUSINESS
An American Place
Artusi
Campagna
Duane Park Café
Four Season's Grill
Judson Grill
La Côte Basque
Le Chantilly
Manhattan Ocean Club
Oceana
Park Avenue Café
Patroon
Picholine
Savoy
Trois Jean

PRIVATE DINING ROOM
"21" Club
Barbetta
Felidia
Four Seasons
La Caravelle
La Grenouille
Le Petit Hulot
Lutèce
Tribeca Grill
Tapika
Patroon
Picholine

SATURDAY LUNCH
Bar Pitti
Downtown
Lobster Club
Osteria del Circo
Becco
Harry Cipriani
Matthew's
Mesa Grill
Sette MoMA
Union Square Cafe
Willow
Zoë

NEW YORK STYLE
"21" Club
Bryant Park
City Wine & Cigar
Gotham Bar & Grill
Grand Central Oyster Bar
Hudson River Club
Maloney & Porcelli
P.J. Clarke's
Rainbow Room
River Café
Spark's Steakhouse
Window's on the World

GRAND CELEBRATION
Aureole
Daniel
Felidia
Four Season's Pool Room
Jean-Georges
Le Bernardin
Le Cirque 2000
Les Célébrités
Lespinasse
Lutèce
Montrachet
San Domenico

INFORMAL CELEBRATION
Alison on Dominick
Bouterin
Follonico
I Trulli
The Independent
JoJo
L'Absinthe
La Goulue
Layla

GETAWAY
Box Tree
Hangawi
Honmura An
Le Colonial
Nobu
Patria
Pravda
Quatorze bis
Sanzin
Sweet Ophelia
Tapas Lounge
Vong

ROMANCE
Arcadia
Café des Artistes
Cascabel
Chanterelle
Chez Josephine
Daniel
Eros
Firebird
King's Carriage House
Pō
Parioli Romanissimo
Verbena

GARDEN
Aureole
Barbetta
Barolo
Home

DESTINATION DINING

I Trulli
Le Petit Hulot
Le Refuge
March
Provence
Restaurant Raphaël
Sea Grill
Verbena

DRINKS
5757
Bar 6
Café 44
Café Centro
Candela
Cub Room
Gramercy Tavern
Match
Monkey Bar
Oak Room & Bar
Rainbow Room
Typhoon Brewey

TAKE-OUT

Bella Blu
Bistro du Nord
Café Evergreen
Caffe Bondí
Carnegie Deli
Caviarteria
Canton
Cha Yen
Chin Chin
China Fun
Cosi Sandwich Bar
Dawat
Ferrara
Ferrier
Gigino
John's of Bleecker
Josie's
Katz's
Kiosk
Les Halles
Layla
Mezze
Mi Cocina
Monsoon
Orienta
Osteria del Circo
Palm, The
Post House
Puket
Rain
Rusty Staub's on Fifth
Shun Lee Palace
Sofia
Soho Kitchen & Bar
Sushi-Say
Sylvia's
Three Guys, The
Trois Jean
Tucci
Vivolo Cucina
Zen Palate
Zeppole

WINNING WINE LISTS

- "21" Club
- Arcadia
- Aureole
- Barolo
- Café Botanico
- Café Evergreen
- Campagna
- Chanterelle
- Cité
- Daniel
- Felidia
- Four Seasons
- Gotham Bar & Grill
- Gramercy Tavern
- Grand Central Oyster Bar
- Hudson River Club
- Judson Grill
- La Caravelle
- Le Bernardin
- Le Périgord
- Les Célébrités
- Lespinasse
- Lutèce
- March
- Maloney & Porcelli
- Manhattan Ocean Club
- Michael's
- Montrachet
- Park Avenue Café
- Patroon
- Post House
- Peacock Alley
- River Café, The
- Rusty Staub's on Fifth
- San Domenico
- Sea Grill
- Sign of the Dove
- Smith & Wollensky
- Sparks Steak House
- Trois Jean
- Union Square Café
- Windows on The World

FUN SPOTS FOR KIDS

- American Festival Café
- Brooklyn Diner
- Canton
- Carmine's
- Carnegie Deli
- China Fun
- EJ's Luncheonette
- Ed Sullivan's
- Empire Diner, The
- Ennio & Michael
- Hard Rock Café
- Harley Davidson Café
- Hosteria Fiorella
- Hot Tomato
- Jerry's
- Mangia e Bevi
- Mesa City
- Mesa Grill
- Mickey Mantle's
- Planet Hollywood
- Redeye Grill
- Royal Canadian Pancake House
- Serendipity
- Sofia
- Tavern on the Green
- Virgil's Barbecue
- World Yacht Cruises

GREAT VALUE

(Fixed prices subject to change)

LUNCH

Price	Restaurant
8.95	Il Vigneto
11.95	Bistro du Nord
12.95	Dawat
13.95	Toscana
14.00	Quatorze bis
14.50	Aqua Grill
14.50	The Odeon
16.00	Honmura An
16.95	Al Bustan
16.95	Becco
17.95	Mirezi
19.50	Picholine
19.50	Le Réfuge
19.96	Ferrier
19.97	Café Luxembourg
19.97	Christer's
19.97	Duane Park Café
19.97	Fraunces Tavern
19.97	Gotham Bar & Grill
19.97	Layla
19.97	Le Chantilly
19.97	Palm
19.97	San Domenico
19.97	Tribeca Grill
19.97	Water Club, The
20.00	Arizona 206
23.00	Café des Artistes
25.00	"21" Club
25.00	JoJo
25.95	Harry Cipriani
26.00	Bouterin
26.00	Tavern on the Green
27.50	Felidia
29.00	Aquavit
32.00	Aureole
32.00	Le Périgord
33.00	Daniel
33.00	Gramercy Tavern
33.00	La Côte Basque
34.00	Oceana
36.00	La Caravelle
38.00	Lutèce

DINNER

(*indicates pre-theater price only)

Price	Restaurant
18.95	Vivolo*
19.50	Indochine*
19.95	Becco*
19.95	Chez Michallet*
19.95	Table d'Hôte*
19.97	Ferrier*
19.97	Scalinatella*
22.95	Osteria Al Doge*
24.95	O'Neal's*
25.00	La Mangeoire
25.00	Pō (five courses)
25.00	Arizona 206*
25.50	L'Ardoise
26.00	Tavern on the Green*
26.50	Café Luxembourg*
28.00	Downtown
29.00	Tropica
29.00	"21" Club*
29.00	Le Chantilly*
29.50	Two Two Two
29.50	Four Seasons Grill
29.50	San Domenico*
29.75	Bruno's Pen & Pencil
31.00	Tapika*
32.00	Montrachet
32.95	Hangawi
32.96	Judson Grill*
33.50	Café Crocodile
34.00	Sign of the Dove*
35.00	Sea Grill*
37.50	Cité*
39.00	March
39.00	Terrace, The
39.00	Barbetta*
39.00	Café 44*
39.00	La Caravelle*
39.00	Sardi's*

CHEAP EATS

(Where a meal should run about $25)

Acme Bar & Grill
Brooklyn Diner
Café Evergreen
Café Lure
China Fun
Col Legno
EJ's Luncheonette
Empire Diner
Frico Bar
Home
Hosteria Fiorella
Il Bagatto
Il Vigneto
J.G. Melon's
Jerry's
Josie's
Katz's Delicatessen
Mangia e Bevi
Mediterraneo
Mi Cocina
Monsoon
Noodle Town
P.J. Clarke's
Pisces
Rain
Right Bank
Sarabeth's Kitchen
Serendipity
Sesso
Soho Steak
Tompkins 131
Tramps Café
Tucci
Virgil's Barbecue

PASSPORT
Vintage Wine Chart

Wine	'82	'83	'84	'85	'86	'87	'88	'89	'90	'91	'92	'93	'94	'95
Beaujolais												8	8.5	9B
Red Bordeaux	10B	8	5	8	9B	7	8B	10B	9A	7B	7B	8B	8A	9A
Red Burgandy	6	9	5	9	7	7	9	9	10B	8B	7B	7A	8A	9A
White Burgandy	6	8	6	8	9	7	8	10	9	7	8	8B	8.5B	9B
Rhône Red	8	9	5	9	8	6	8	9B	9B	8B	7B	8B	8.5B	9A
Baralo	9	8	5	10	7	7	8B	9B	9B	7	6	8B	8A	9A
Chianti							8	9	9	7	7B	7B	8B	9A
Cabernet Sauvignon	7	7	9	9	9	9	7	7	9A	9A	9A	9B	9A	9A
Chardonnay							8	8	9	8	8	9	9B	9B

Select Vintages

Sauternes	'90A '89A '88A '86B '85 '83 '76 '75 '71 '67
German Wine	'92 '91 '90 '89 '88 '85 '82 '79 '76 '71
Champagne	'90 '89 '86 '85 '83 '82 '79 '76
Classic Claret	'78 '75 '70 '66 '61 '59 '55 '53 '49 '47 '45
Vintage Port	'92A '91A '85B '83B '80B '77B '75 '70 '66 '63

A = needs more Aging
B = drinkable now, but could Benefit from more aging